Praise for
Follow Through: A Swing For Life

"*Medicine for the soul! Kerwin Owens has written practical wisdom that takes you from stumbling to start something to FOLLOWING THROUGH TO FINISHING! The stories are fun, tearjerking and stimulating: AND PRACTICAL! The cover should be made of Golf shoe leather because the insight is so practical and will help you walk through the course of life with impact and purpose! It is wisdom from God...BUY IT NOW AND FOLLOW THROUGH TO THE FINISH!*

–Don Johnson, CEO and Founder, Difference Makers

"*I am not much of a golfer, but I know when someone is on fire for God. Kerwin's insight and guidance in this book is on fire. He has brilliantly intertwined spirituality through the game of golf for all of us to Follow Through in a more intimate relationship with God in all we do. If you wish to know God on a deeper level, I dare you to read Follow Through. You too, will be on fire!*"

–Mickey Washington, Former NFL Player, and Attorney & CEO of Washington & Associates, PLLC

"Great stories can be appreciated when one can truly relate and connect to the messages in the bible. Kerwin has done a phenomenal job in drawing the analogies of golf and life, to truly articulate God's Word. This is a MUST read!"

–Gentry Humphrey, Former Vice President of
Nike Jordan Footwear and Owner of CODE

"I've known Kerwin since before his birth and throughout his entire life. I mentored him, anticipating his significant contribution of work on earth to people, and I'm honored to be featured in his remarkable book, Follow Through. Having read it, and even helped him write it, I believe it's his finest work yet—an absolute must read."

–God, your dad, and Paul, the author of
Ephesians 2:10

FOLLOW THROUGH

A SWING FOR LIFE

KERWIN OWENS

First Edition

Published by:
KO Key Optimization Coaching, LLC
eMail: kokeyopt@outlook.com
Instagram: @kokeyoptimizationcoaching

Book Cover and Interior Design by:
Jessica Tilles/TWASolutions.com

ISBN: 979-8-218-32843-6

Scriptures taken from The ESV Bible (The Holy Bible, English Standard Version) Text Edition: 2016, Copyright 2011 by Crossway, a publishing ministry of Good News Publishers.

Printed in the United States of America

Distributed by IngramContent
www.ingramcontent.com

To Demetris, my wife, my inspiration, my constant support and love for twenty-five years. Here's to following through together. With God at our center, we've journeyed through life's twists and turns, always striving to follow through in His grace.

TABLE OF CONTENTS

MEET ME INSIDE THE CLUBHOUSE

"All authority in heaven and on earth has been given to me.
Therefore, go and make disciples of all nations…and teach them
to obey everything I have commanded you. And surely I am
with you always, to the very end of the age."
–Matthew 28:18-20

"Allow me to introduce myself."

I often begin conversations with this phrase when I meet people I do not know at the golf clubhouse. This opening greeting is a common occurrence for millions of people every day who meet people they do not know. During a typical round of golf, which can take on average anywhere from four to five hours to play eighteen holes, we would have ample

1

time to get to know each other. This amount of time spent together with people offers excellent chances for meaningful interactions.

I'll learn more about them, and they'll learn more about me.

Since you will spend the next several hours of your time reading my viewpoints on following through, it's only fair I share a little about myself. I am a child of God, a husband to my beautiful wife, Demetris, for twenty-five years, and a father to three amazing kids: Devin, Demi, and Kennedy, who also know God. I love God. I love my family. I love people. And I love golf. My follow-through is the only reason this book is in your possession.

As an avid golfer for over twenty-five years, I've learned many things about the game of golf and life. One of the most fascinating things I've learned, and the reason I've written this book, is that there are many facets of the game of golf—the stance, the swing, and the mental aspect—that are great metaphors for principles of life I aspire to follow.

I have had my fair share of low-scoring rounds, and, unfortunately, some high. In life, I've had some lows and highs as well. More importantly, I have had countless amazing experiences both in golf and life, and across the world, connecting with people and learning their stories as they have learned about mine. We all have a story. In this book, you will read some of those stories—whether they're mine, ones

I've heard on a golf course, from family and friends, or from resources like books, articles, or social media.

I will guide you through the process of the golf swing, various golf shots, and the golf experiences I've had, as well as those of others. I'll then draw connections between these aspects of the golf swing and the spiritual insights that have been inspired through and breathed out by God's Word.

The follow-through phase represents one of the most graceful postures of a golf swing. It continues the motion of a golf swing to completion after hitting the golf ball. The follow-through can sometimes be one of the most challenging not just in golf, but also in various other sports or personal activities, depending on the task at hand. However, if completed properly, it can also be very rewarding. Whether it's in personal or work relationships, following through is really significant. Doing so can help you build a good reputation or, if you don't, it may harm your credibility.

It is my aspiration that this book supports you in pursuing and achieving your dreams, goals, and tasks by utilizing the tools I'll provide, which I have gained from studying God's Word, and from personal experiences, also known as wisdom.

The idea of *The Transformational Power of the Follow Through* didn't just drop out of the sky. It was a thought teed up in my heart and soul by the Holy Spirit. This thought encouraged me to draw a correlation between golf swing mechanics and life principles. Using metaphorical language,

I will guide you on a journey from the clubhouse to the golf range, then onto the course, and ultimately back to the clubhouse. Throughout this journey, I will delve into prevalent swing mechanics and sayings in golf, correlating them with life principles and linking them to deeply meaningful scriptures. This exploration will revolve around the four phases of a golf swing: The Set-Up, Trust, Commit, and Follow Through.

I hope to give you as much direction and clarity with how to accept and take on life's most rewarding blessings, as well as help you prepare and manage life's most challenging difficulties. If you're not familiar with golf, my hope remains the same: that, much like I anticipate from avid golfers, you grasp the bigger picture of how to fulfill God's purpose in your life, reinforcing His teachings and guidance, which were communicated to us over two thousand years ago through His Word.

I hope you enjoy reading this as much as I enjoyed writing it. My goal is to perhaps help you get better at golf, if you play, however, I would love for you to improve your life by following through and accomplishing what you most desire, and achieving what you want—something I believe God would love to see! Let's get it!

THE SET UP

Let's Hit the Range

"You will definitely enjoy what you've worked hard for—
you'll be happy; and things will go well for you."

–Psalm 128:2

1. *Wake up to a four-mile jog*
2. *Go to the gym to lift weights*
3. *Two to three hours of range practice*
4. *Play some holes*
5. *Return to work on short game*
6. *Run another four miles*
7. *Play basketball or tennis, if the option is there*

The above used to be a typical day for Tiger Woods. Claimed to be two of the hardest workers in the golf sport in their golf careers, Tiger and Vijay Singh had a goal in mind: to win as many tournaments as they participated in.

Fans of golf watched them achieve many of those goals over the years.

"Many" to the tune of Tiger having tied the record with Sam Snead for the most wins ever in the history of golf on the PGA tour at 82 and counting, while Vijay has 34 wins ranked #14 in the top 20 as of April 16, 2023, according to PGA Tour. Hard work and preparation are a great combination when the opportunity presents itself. It's a beautiful thing to see.

On the flip side, not working hard or being lazy has its consequences, too. You could experience limited achievement, career stagnation, financial struggles, challenges in personal growth, relational strain, health issues, missed opportunities, and regret, just to name a few. I believe Proverbs 6:10-11 says it best, *"A little extra sleep, a little more slumber, a little folding of the hands to rest, and poverty will pounce on you like a bandit; scarcity will attack you like an armed robber."*

When you're getting ready for success, whether preparing for a golf round, launching your own business, climbing the corporate ladder, working hard to get a bachelor's degree, or gearing up to play a sport of your liking, hard work is required. You will have to make sacrifices. Hard work comes with a cost. A cost of energy. A cost of time. In some cases, the cost of having fun. If you think the cost of working hard is high, wait until you get the bill for regret. There is no substitute for hard work.

I share with my kids all the time: you can work hard, or you can work harder, but be sure to commit your work to

God and your plans will be established. Proverbs 16:3 says, *"Commit your actions to the Lord, and your plans will succeed."* Even the writing of this book to research and communicate what I believe are key essentials in how to live a life pleasing and acceptable to God is hard work. However, the fruit of my labor is priceless. The "fruit" being prayerfully that at least one person finds encouragement in some form by reading this book. That's fruitful to me and all glory be to God for it. As it says in Psalms 128:2, *"You shall eat the fruit of the labor of your hands; you shall be blessed, and it shall be well with you."* You will enjoy the fruit of your labor. It's God's promise. How joyful and prosperous you will be!

Work hard in all things. It's essential to remember that hard work doesn't guarantee success in every aspect of your life, but it significantly increases your chances of achieving your goals and leading a more fulfilling life. Hard work will pay off in some way, shape, form, or fashion. I believe it! You should, too. Trust God. Trust the process!

There are many reasons we spend time on the golf practice range before a round of golf. It could simply be to warm up the different body muscles used during your golf swing or ensure you are able to hit any of your golf clubs consistently and accurately a certain distance and location targeted when required at any given time. It could also be to boost your confidence and strengthen your mental, and many other things. To a golfer, the practice range does not differ from anyone preparing for an interview for a job, or a presentation someone has to pitch to their class or co-workers. The bottom line is, preparation is key to the execution of a plan. It's one of many steps in having the proper set-up of a short- or long-term goal.

Similar to Tiger Woods, and over half my life, I have established a daily routine where the first part of my day, whether ten minutes or thirty minutes, I spend time with God through reading His Word and prayer. It is intentional in my preparation or set-up to set me mentally and spiritually up for a successful day. I begin with thankfulness for waking me up in the morning, my health, for a roof over our heads, my family, and small things as simple as food and water that I take for granted. This gratitude puts things into perspective despite any challenges I may face at that moment. Afterward, I head to the gym and spend about an hour working on my body, believing and hoping that my body will continue to give me the ability to enjoy my family, my friends, and, of course, golf! Then, I'll go to work and put the time in needed to fulfill that assignment in the electrical engineering space, before making my way home to have dinner and the rest of the evening with my family until bedtime.

Except for the time with God and family, this schedule is hard work. With God's help, all of it works together for the good of my family and me. Over the years, spending that time reading and meditating on God's Word in the morning before the start of my day has prepared me for some amazing wins and losses in all areas of my life. Just like working on your golf swing technique multiple times on the golf range before a round of golf or in-between golf rounds is huge to knowing the right club for the right yardage when facing that shot on the golf course. Repetitions in reading key scriptures in the Bible are pivotal, as there are always moments that will require you to lean on scripture to help you through that moment. That's the best preparation you can get that will pay huge dividends!

While on the range, as golfers set up for their golf round, they will ensure that all required clubs are in the golf bag. Golfers also confirm they have the right clubs, from the driver to the sand wedge to the putter, which will allow them to hit every shot during their round of golf. Of course, they make sure they wear the right golf gear; the right golf shoes that fit their personality, a nice belt, and the proper cap that's appealing to them.

Keeping that same check and balance in mind, and as a man of God, I also make sure I'm spiritually prepared for my day as I'm spending my time with God in the morning. I've placed on the proper gear so I can make it through the day.

When my kids were younger, I recall asking them, "Do you ever go to school without your shoes on? Have you ever gone to school barefoot?"

Their responses were pretty quick, almost in unison, with an outburst of laughter. "No, Dad, that's silly!"

I used that to bring my point home—never leave home without putting on the full armor of God as He has taught us in His Word. A golfer not hitting the range is taking a big risk of looking silly out on the course, just like a kid going to school in bare feet. Of course, there is a legitimate risk of injuring yourself walking without shoes. There is a risk of not winning a PGA tournament without hitting the range. There is a significant risk of behaving out of Christ-like character without putting on the full armor of God in so many ways. Just like preparing for a round of golf, ensuring to equip yourself with the proper golf equipment for obstacles presented to you, it's that much more important to be equipped with the teachings God provides to help you.

Honestly, it's beneficial for you as well to have God in your heart while you're on the golf course. This can assist you in handling your performance both mentally and physically while you're playing. God provides comfort when you're experiencing discomfort and clarity when your thoughts may be foggy, especially to make important decisions. He gives me everything I need when I need it. His timing is amazing in delivering answers to my most difficult questions.

As it says in Ephesians 6:13-18, *"Therefore, put on the full armor of God, so that when the day of evil comes, you may be able to stand your ground, and after you have done everything, to stand. Stand firm then, with the belt of truth buckled around your waist, with the breastplate of righteousness in place, and with your feet fitted with the readiness that comes from the gospel of peace. In addition to all this, take up the shield of faith, with which you can extinguish all the flaming arrows of the evil one. Take the helmet of salvation and the sword of the Spirit, which is the word of God. And pray in the Spirit on all occasions with all kinds of prayers and requests."*

With this in mind, be alert and always keep on praying for all the Lord's people. This applies to setting up for the day, as well as setting up to play a round of golf! Work hard and be prepared for what life may bring. Get that range time in! Put the work in those areas that matter most to you. You will see the fruit of your labor as God has promised. It may not always be exactly what you are expecting, but it will be what is best for you. Anything God gives you is so much better than what you can give yourself. Know one thing: God never stops working.

What disciplines can you incorporate in your life to help maintain your consistency and dedication in your efforts to study and apply God's Word in your daily life? _____

_____

_____

_____

_____

How will you gain a deeper understanding of God's Word and stimulate your spiritual growth? _____

_____

_____

_____

_____

_____

_____

Keeping the concept of "faith without works is dead" in mind, how can you apply this idea to the notion of putting in effort to study and live according to God's Word? What implications does this hold for your life as a believer? _____

_____

_____

_____

_____

In which aspect of your life could you put in more effort to either improve or achieve a set goal? _____

_____

_____

_____

_____

THE SET UP

Positioned Well?

"But seek first the kingdom of God and his righteousness,
and all these things will be added to you."

–Matthew 6:33

"Today, I will do what others won't, so tomorrow I can
do what others can't."
– Jerry Rice, American Former Football Player

Sacrifices and decisions you make today can impact your life tomorrow in your health, your career, your finances, and/or your relationships.

If you ever get to a level in golf where you're playing it like the game of chess, you have arrived. Let me explain.

Imagine you're on the golf course, standing on hole #2 and it's a short par 4 that plays 400 yards from tee to green and you're standing on the tee box. As you scan the hole and take a peek at the flag, you then scan to your right and left to see trees on both sides of the fairway. You also notice bunkers on both sides of the fairway. However, neither of these hazards concerns you because you know you have a club in the bag you can use to hit the ball so it can land well beyond those bunkers on either side.

It would be fun and an adrenaline rush to hit the driver club from the tee which is the club any golfer can hit the longest distance generally speaking. Unfortunately, as a result of choosing this club you take the risk of hitting your ball in the trees on either side of the fairway as a driver club is the least forgiving compared to all the other golf clubs in your golf bag in terms of hitting a ball straight. If you're having a good day on the course, perhaps you hit the golf ball an extremely long way down the middle of the fairway and leave yourself 40 yards from the flag. In the event you're in the fairway in the latter scenario, it would be amazing if your short game from 40 yards or less from the green is second to none. If not, you're in a tough position.

With the outcome of those two scenarios not being favorable, it would be wise and a great decision to hit an easier club off the tee whether it is a long iron or a fairway wood that will place you 120 to 130 yards out from the green to put a pitching wedge in your hands for your next shot. The pitching wedge is one of your favorite clubs for sure, and you can always put the ball within a five to eight feet circle around the flag stick on the green. This is a good example of thinking ahead to place you in the best position to be successful.

The same strategy applies in all areas of our life. What decisions can you make today that will positively manifest itself at a later time in the future? I recall sitting in church one Sunday morning with my wife over twenty-three years ago. She was pregnant with our first child. On this day, we knew we were having a boy. So, as we sat in church, I had been pondering on boy names for a while. Then suddenly, it hit me square in the face.

During the sermon, the minister told the story of a man who was a chief tax collector named Zacchaeus, who was wealthy, short in stature, and wanted to see Jesus, the Messiah. He simply wanted to have an opportunity to see him in person on a day when he knew he would be walking down this one road.

As he and many others gathered at a specific location just off the road, and a path they expected Jesus to walk down, the area became extremely crowded. This made it almost impossible for Zacchaeus to see Him because of his height, since he was short compared to many of the people also there who wanted to see and meet Jesus.

Zacchaeus thought about it and came up with an amazing idea. He decided to run ahead of this location and climb a nearby sycamore-fig tree just off the road that placed him in the ideal position to catch a great view of Jesus based on the path he expected Him to walk.

When Jesus finally walked by this tree, He looked up in the tree and noticed Zacchaeus and called him by name. He told him to come down because He was going to his house. Zacchaeus hurriedly climbed down and received Jesus joyfully. Ultimately, Zacchaeus' life was changed as he repented of his sins and gave his life to Christ.

Zacchaeus had placed himself in the ultimate position! Zacchaeus put himself into a position of humility and submission to Christ. A position Jesus recognized, honored, and responded to Zacchaeus changing his life here on Earth and eternally after life on Earth.

What a position to be in! Make a solid effort to experience Jesus in your life and you will be rewarded. Seek Him with all your heart and do everything He would have you do! It was clear to me, after hearing this story, my son's name will be Devin Zacchaeus Owens. My wife and I wanted a name for our child to be connected in some way to God, to honor and thank Him for giving us a baby, as well as ask for His blessing on Devin for his life at the same time. It's amazing how God works full circle over twenty-four years later to use this personal experience to bring home a point of using Zacchaeus' story to provide an example of being positioned well. Crazy how God works sometimes.

In golf, it is a commonly coined phrase that when a ball is in the middle of the fairway, the golfer is in position "A." This means relative to position "B" or "C," it only gets worse where your next shot is limited, like behind a tree, or in the lip of a fairway bunker. These other positions are less than favorable and not much you can do with hitting the golf ball.

I love how my good friend, Gentry Humphrey, former Vice President of Nike Jordan Footwear and Owner of Footwear company, CODE, says, "Whenever you come from an authentic position, you can do whatever you want to do!" In golf, if you're in position "A" or an "authentic" position, you can fade the ball or draw it from the middle of the fairway. You also have the option to put a spin on the ball or play a bump and run shot to force it to spin or release to the pin, respectively, when the ball lands on the green.

When you're in an open fairway, you have the flexibility to choose among many options as you don't have limitations, like that of your ball being behind a tree.

Gentry expounded on his thought of authenticity and said, "Being your 'authentic self', with ethical principles, you are allowed to operate in a space that is truly grounded in the essence of what is real and in what is your truth. Knowing this, you should feel comfortable being uncomfortable! While stepping in uncharted space can be difficult for some, you can become that beacon of light that shows others alternative ways of reaching success." I would add to Gentry's statement that "When you are your authentic self, which is how God designed you specifically, He will do His best work through you. It will position you well to hit some of your best shots!" Meaning, you are equipped with God's gifts to do some of your best work.

"For we are God's handiwork, created in Christ Jesus for good works, which God prepared in advance for us to do," Ephesians 2:10. Be your authentic self and do what God has already laid out for you to do. Be yourself because everybody else is taken. It will be fulfilling!

Decisions can also be critical. Faith-based decisions versus fleshly, where poor decisions result in painful consequences. Translation: Allowing the Holy Spirit to lead you versus your physical flesh, where it may seem fun or feeling-based that are immoral, impure, jealous, or angry, to name a few. These acts can be costly to you and likely to others around you. My advice here is to study and meditate on Galatians 5:16, where Paul states, *"But I say, walk by the Spirit, and you will not gratify the desires of the flesh."* To walk in a Godly way, you must get yourself in a close relationship with God and His Word to know and understand how and what to do. Let him lead you in your decisions at all times. Be sensitive and alert.

We make decisions every minute of the day that can impact the trajectory of the path of our lives, be it our health, our finances, our relationships, and many other things, for good or bad. David says, in Proverbs 3:6, *"In all your ways acknowledge him, and he will make straight your paths."* God will help us in our decision-making if we ask Him. With God-led decisions, He will place us right where He wants us to be, in the perfect position to do His best work through us. It will be rewarding to both Him and us beyond our imagination.

Making good choices to position your ball in a round of golf is a game-changer! We have heard that the golf course has to be managed. Know where the hazards are off the tee. Understand where the bunkers are relative to the flag. Understanding what side of the flag to target puts you in a position to putt uphill versus downhill. It can be the difference between putting three times versus one due to the level of difficulty. There are many other things to consider before just swinging away. Hit golf shots that position you well for the second. Make decisions today that will have an impact on you tomorrow. Making decisions with God first is a game changer as well!

Then there is a time when we have good intentions, but we cannot execute. We're human. We didn't hit the ball we intended, and it did not quite land on the course where we wanted it to. We have seen some of the greatest players on the PGA Tour ever to play the game, be creative just like Tiger, and somehow pull off golf shots when it seems impossible. It's always fun to watch a golf pro find a difficult lie, whether when they find their ball with mud on it, or their ball lands in a divot in the middle of the fairway, or behind a tree. They make some adjustments to their swing and pull off a shot that's often spectacular. Some of these have been practiced before, whereas some have not.

Control what we can and trust God to control what we cannot. For example, set up that meal plan and have healthy food choices always available at your fingertips. Plan ahead. Make them easily accessible. Now, when you get hungry or when something jumps on your calendar and forces you to pivot from your original lunch or dinner plans, you don't have to rush and eat something unhealthy because of time constraints. You just mitigated the risk of eating unhealthy.

You will inevitably miss your target, whether in golf or some other personal or professional endeavor. We're not perfect on the golf course, nor are we perfect in our lives off the golf course when faced with decisions we must make. We must improvise frequently or adjust to put us back in a good position. What adjustments must you make to execute a plan to get back on track and put you back in a good position? Seek God's wisdom and guidance in whatever situation you've found yourself in. All things are possible if you put Him first and trust and believe in Him, and you'll be positioned well in an authentic way that may and likely could change your life!

Are you currently in the optimal position both personally and professionally? _____

_____

_____

_____

_____

_____

_____

_____

Are you in an authentic position? _____

_____

_____

_____

_____

_____

_____

_____

What beliefs might you have that limit your potential? What steps will you take to achieve an advantageous position? ___

_____

_____

_____

_____

_____

MULLIGAN

The Prodigal Son

*"[13]Not many days later, the younger son gathered all he
had and took a journey into a far country, and there he
squandered his property in reckless living. [21]And the son said
to him, 'Father, I have sinned against heaven and you. I
am no longer worthy to be called your son. [22]But the father
said to his servants, 'Bring quickly the best robe, and put it
on him, and put a ring on his hand, and shoes on his feet.
[23]And bring the fattened calf and kill it, and let us eat and
celebrate. For this my son was dead, and is alive again; he
was lost, and is found.' And they began to celebrate."*

—Luke 15:11-30

I magine this: you have the opportunity to play a round of golf
anywhere in the world. In addition to that, you also have a
choice to pick the three most important or influential people
in your life that either you're a huge fan of or someone who
has had the biggest impact in your life to make up your dream

foursome. It could even be a loved one that may have passed away and have gone before us.

The point of the exercise is to identify three individuals that you will play a round of golf with, to spend up to four and one-half hours on the most beautiful course in the world. This is the opportunity of a lifetime that will allow you to share with them what they mean to you, get to know them better, and for them to get to know you.

You're now on the opening golf hole of this golf round and it's now your time to hit the first tee shot. You're focused and super nervous, but anxious to hit the ball to help with getting the jitters out of what will be a magical day! Sure enough, you hit it, and it soars to the right, without a doubt, straight into the trees.

First off, you're in denial, telling yourself you could not believe you just did that in front of the three most influential people that you highly admire. You process it a little further in the next few seconds and then feel embarrassed. Then someone in your dream foursome, with the most gentle voice, yells loud enough for you to hear them, "Take a Mulligan KO!" It is like music to your ears!

In that one statement, you experience grace and mercy, compassion, empathy, and so many other feelings that simply make you whole. You've been granted a second chance, without affecting your score. A Mulligan is simply a second chance where the first swing does not count. It's a free golf shot!

The definition of a Mulligan is a second chance to perform an action, usually after the first chance went wrong through bad luck or a blunder. Its best-known use is in golf, whereby it refers to a player being allowed, only informally, to replay a stroke, although that is against the formal rules of golf. It's usually provided by friends whose desire is for you to start off well.

I'm honestly writing this chapter as a good friend of mine, Anna Baldwin, asked, after I explained a summary of what this book is about, "What about those people who are lost? What about those individuals, including people of faith, that have lost their way?" It was the most profound question, and with all sincerity, I did not have a good answer. I further thought about the word "lost" in golf and what happens to a golfer when they experience loss. It's most painfully felt when, on the tee box, the golfer hits the ball either in the water, the rough, or in the trees, and the golf ball is lost. It's one of the worst feelings any golfer can have during a round of golf, particularly on the first tee!

As I thought about the use of Mulligans on occasions to cover or replace a lost ball, and ultimately reset the round for that individual back to start, I thought, *What if God had a golf course?* I'd imagine, based on His promises and what He has communicated to those who believe in Him, He would have limitless Mulligans, no out-of-bounds marked off, and no penalties incurred ever during a round of golf, regardless of how horrible a golf shot hit.

On His golf course, you'll never have a lost ball. In your life, as you live it now, as a believer in Him, you'll always have Him to help you find your way back to Him, reconnecting and rekindling your relationship with Him. However, at times, we do still feel lost or far away from God, because of a multitude of reasons—loss of a loved one, a job loss, a break-up in a relationship, or simply not confident, nor seeing value in yourself. It happens many times and for many reasons.

It would be a challenge to explain when, how, and why this happens, but it does. What I can tell you, based on research, is that when we do experience loss, we experience denial, anger or frustration, bargaining, depression, and eventually acceptance. I will also tell you that the further you are away from God, the more intense and painful these feelings are. The closer you are to God, the less intense and painful it is.

Grief is a complex and unique journey for each individual. We'll discuss in this chapter how you may experience these feelings in your life when dealing with either feeling lost, losing something, or someone valuable to you, and ways to cope with it. No matter what, please know this as it says in Psalm 34:18, *"The Lord is close to the brokenhearted and saves those who are crushed in spirit."* This verse reminds us that even in our darkest moments, God is near and offers support and healing to those who are hurting.

Denial can be deadly! You are in disbelief or shock that what just happened actually happened! Whether hitting a ball in the middle of the lake, or into the trees, it's difficult to accept the reality. Denial is a protective mechanism in the initial stages of experiencing the pain or disappointment of losing.

I've experienced this in multiple areas of my life where I simply want to protect my heart and mind from the reality of loss, be it in sports, in relationships, or my career. The good news is that I've also found a way of coping with the losses in my life through my relationship with God.

Matthew 5:4 encourages us to mourn when appropriate and in the right way. It says, *"Blessed are those who mourn, for they shall be comforted."* He didn't say specifically who and how, but you shall be comforted. I now keep an open heart and mind to receive positive people or anything that will add value to my life while providing comfort, whether through conversations or activities with balance.

When my father passed now eight years ago, a scripture I keep close to my heart is Isiah 41:10, *"Fear not, for I am with you; be not dismayed, for I am your God; I will strengthen you, I will help you, I will uphold you with my righteous right hand."* You can use that for not only a loss in your life, but for anything you feel the need for His support. God makes it clear in this verse; He's got you!

I also lean on Psalm 147:3, "*He heals the broken-hearted and binds up their wounds.*" When He heals and binds up, it's complete and will not re-open. Thank God. I believe the challenge in the "denial" phase is to face reality as quickly as possible to get the process going and move through the grieving phase, as this could be one of many phases if you find yourself going through all of them. We're not perfect. We're all broken. God heals and takes care of His.

God says, in Matthew 11:28-30, "*Come to me, all who labor and are heavy laden, and I will give you rest. Take my yoke upon you, and learn from me, for I am gentle and lowly in heart, and will find rest for your souls. For my yoke is easy, and my burden is light.*" Give it to Him!

The next phase of loss is anger. This one is a beast! I have blurted out during a round of golf after a short putt missed, or a golf ball hit and entered the center of a lake, resulting in a penalty stroke. I've also experienced a level of frustration that impacted the rest of my golf round, or golf hole to an extent where it made matters worse—not only for me, but for others around me. The same happens in life with family members or close friends who are now experiencing you as someone quite different and not fun to be around as you deal with loss in certain areas of your life where it truly impacts your outlook on life.

James 1:19-20 gives great advice on how to handle anger in things as simple as a conversation. *"Let every person be quick to hear, slow to speak, slow to anger; for the anger of man does not produce the righteousness of God."* In summary, nothing good comes out of anger! Have both humility and respect for others. Don't allow the devil to ruin a good round of golf or your relationship with others.

Truly take the appropriate time to allow yourself to get to a place of calmness in your mind, spirit, and heart to ensure you don't say or do something you'll regret all because of being in a state of anger where you are not thinking logically. It's a good investment to have that self-awareness and connect with your inner spirit.

Colossians 3:8 gives specific directions to *"...put them all away: anger, wrath, malice, slander, and obscene talk from your mouth."* We're human. We make mistakes and things happen. Recover, refocus, and operate out of love, controlling how we respond. God will bless us in our response and help us along the way. He's equipped us appropriately!

How many times have we lost a ball, be it with hitting a ball with the driver off the tee, or hitting a ball with a fairway wood or iron off the fairway? We begin talking to ourselves, rationalizing and negotiating if we would have done something different in our swing, like if we stayed in the slot, we wouldn't be looking in the trees or starring in the middle of the lake. Only "if" statements show up all the time when we wish we could have said or done something different.

I can't tell you how many times I wish I could take back statements I'd said to my wife during our twenty-five years of marriage that unfortunately I simply can't do. The intent of negotiating with my wife after poor statements is an attempt to regain control, to create a loving environment or perhaps finish a great date that was on the right track. When we miss amazing opportunities to create long-lasting, loving memories like that of a beautiful night out with the wife, It's only natural to negotiate to try to save it somehow, but often can be challenging.

Again, this is a phase of grieving the loss of something or someone valuable to you by bargaining and attempting to regain control. As Christians, you gain self-control by trusting and depending on God. We do this through His teaching in Galatians 5:22-23, *But the fruit of the spirit is love, joy, peace, kindness, goodness, faithfulness, gentleness, self-control, against such things there is no law.* When we practice self-control, we are living in obedience to God's Word. Be led by the spirit. Pray and ask God for help and to give you strength. Self-control is the fruit of the spirit. It's a gift from God. Just ask for it! Our behavior will only get better over time, reducing and making fewer mistakes and having more self-control the more we spend time with God and trust Him. Doing this ultimately helps us eliminate and not need to bargain or negotiate, or get through these phases much quicker and without damage to ourselves, the situation, or those around us.

The last two phases are depression and acceptance. The deep sadness of loss is real, whether a person or a thing. A lost golf ball is one thing during a round of golf, but the loss of someone or something valuable can be overwhelming.

Everyone experiences loss differently and may not go through all stages discussed in this chapter. My encouragement is that if you find yourself in a deep sadness or depression, reach out to someone with whom you trust and share your experience. It's best not to isolate yourself from loved ones and to connect with God in parallel. God places people in our lives for a purpose. God loves you. He has placed people in your life for a reason and a season. God is in control of all things, of how they take place, and when. He's God and we're not.

I would encourage you to lean on God. Accept what you cannot control and control what you can with God's guidance. Just like the prodigal son, God will always be there for you, accepting you just as you are regardless of how big the mistakes were or the severity of the circumstances. He's a loving God with open arms, waiting with the finest gifts to forgive and accept you. He wants to do more with you in your life. You can never out-sin God's forgiveness. It's never too late, and God will grant you a Mulligan and allow you to reset!

Do you feel close to God? If not, why? _____

_____

_____

_____

_____

_____

In times of uncertainty, what strategies can help you gain a sense of direction? _____

_____

_____

_____

_____

_____

What activities can you incorporate in your life that will ensure you don't get lost or help you find your way back (i.e., like a GPS finder is to a person when traveling)? _____

_____

_____

_____

_____

_____

THE SET UP

Balanced?
Are Your Feet Set Appropriately Apart?

"My son, pay attention to what I say; turn your ear to my words. Do not let them out of your sight, keep them within your heart; for they are life to those who find them and health to one's whole body. Above all else, guard your heart, for everything you do flows from it."
—Proverbs 4:20-23

How many times have you changed the distance between your feet during your golf career? Has it worked out for you? Did you think it made a difference? Setting your feet appropriately apart will vary the stability and power of your swing. It defines how balanced your stance is relative to the power of your swing. There is a distinct difference in distance between your two feet when chipping around the greens versus standing on the tee box with a driver in your hand looking 300 yards down the fairway at your target point.

Whether it's a short shot or long, setting your feet will determine your balance, with the core of your body being the center of control. In the most basic sense, your core helps you maintain good stability and control throughout the golf swing. Keeping a stable core allows for a very fluid and consistent swing. It is also one of the main areas in which we generate the force needed to hit the ball long distances. Do not understate the importance of core stability to the golf swing.

I lived in Shanghai, China, for six months, working for General Motors in 2004. As a young electrical engineer gaining vertical height in my career, I elected to accept an international special project to develop and mentor engineers in the Asia-Pacific rim while assisting the supply base manufacturing product for General Motors.

What a fascinating place! Also fascinating was the office building where I worked in the city of Pudong, called the Jin Mao. It had ninety-three floors and was the third tallest building in the world. As it relates to balance, it was astonishing that on the 92nd floor was a gyroscope, a device used for measuring and maintaining orientation and angular velocity. It spins in which the axis of rotation is free to assume any orientation by itself. Bottom line, with engineering jargon aside, it was the core of this massive structure to help the building maintain balance. The gyroscope looked to be the size of Jupiter, with chains keeping it suspended in mid-air.

There was also a pool on the 57th floor that acted as a damper, which was also eye-opening. The gyroscope, along with the pool of water's job, was to keep the Jin Mao building balanced no matter the energy or outside elements.

What does your core look like in your golf stance? Are you balanced and have strength in all positions of your golf swing? Is your core strong enough to serve its purpose throughout the swing?

I recall my golf instructor, Lynn Stone, coaching a part of my swing as I was not distributing my body weight properly, losing strength, and ultimately distance with my driver as well as my iron game, and it was challenging. As he would catch my swing on the follow-through during golf lessons, he would ask me to hold it at the top. While holding this pose, I didn't realize what was to come next when he took my hands, while at the top of my follow-through, and reinforced the swing by continuing my arms and hands on its existing path, causing me to lose balance.

He would laugh under his breath as he knew something was not set up properly, whether it was my feet not set appropriately apart from one another, or my core not centered and properly balanced in my current stance that caused me to lose balance. After a couple more times and watching him laugh his heart out, I finally figured out what adjustments I needed to make to ensure balance.

In life, it's the same. We must have and maintain balance. Just like the Jin Mao building is built to withstand unpredictable times when high winds come, or when earthquakes may occur, as Christians, the core of our being has to be strong enough to withstand the unexpected. Expect the unexpected. It starts and begins with the core, our heart and soul.

For me, as a believer, the core of my body, mind, and soul is God. God is in me through His Holy Spirit, who will always be there in the center of my being, providing the best stability, balance, and guidance. As it says in 1 Corinthians 6:19, "*Do you know that your bodies are temples of the Holy Spirit, who is in you, whom you have received from God? You are not your own...*"

You will stand the test of time if you truly believe, trust, and follow Him. When accepting God in your life, He will provide the Holy Spirit to you to be the core of your being, to help you with balance in your life, just as John 14: 26 says, "*But the advocate, the Holy Spirit, whom the Father will send in my name, will teach you all things and will remind you of everything I have said to you.*"

The way to build that core properly is by reading and studying His Word. Perhaps attending church or Bible study can help build an understanding, knowledge, and wisdom of God, which will further strengthen your core or Holy Spirit within you. Learning how to listen and hear His Holy Spirit will help as well.

God is an equalizer and can stabilize any situation, no matter how big or how small. The Holy Spirit is a divine force that can withstand all forces and its influence of God is over the universe and all of mankind. Talk about core strength, balance, and an excellent foundation!

Just as a solid foundation—achieved by properly positioning your feet—is essential for a successful golf swing, similarly, centering your being around God will establish the groundwork for a purposeful and amazing life. Proverbs 24:3-4 says, *"By wisdom a house is built, and by understanding it is established; by knowledge the rooms are filled with all precious and pleasant riches."* God will bless your life. There is so much more He wants to do through you.

God has blessed me with great parents and grandparents who instilled in me His Word, along with teaching me good morals and values, and how I should behave. That upbringing and guidance are truly the root of who I am today. To have respect and be kind to people, love and care for people, and be nice to others as you would want them to be to you.

Biblical scriptures were taught and passed down from one generation to the next, starting with my grandparents on both sides of my parents' families. I'm convinced this strong foundation still drives who I have become and what I believe in today. It further proves to me the strength and longevity of a strong, well-built foundation, standing on the shoulders of my parents and grandparents.

Here's a fun fact relative to the foundation established over two generations ago in my family line on both sides of my family. My paternal grandfather was a pastor for forty-five years in a church I grew up in. I learned recently that my mom's grandfather, who was a carpenter, built the church he pastored. Talk about a foundation that I currently stand on today in my ministry that began years ago.

It reminds me of a verse in the song "The Church I Grew Up In" by Tasha Cobbs. In this song, Tasha eloquently describes, in a beautiful voice, the details of the church she grew up in, encompassing both the exterior and interior. She seamlessly transitions to recounting experiences she has held onto for years, illustrating how healing was present within the church walls. She speaks of angels overseeing her childhood, providing insight into the foundation of her identity and the reasons behind who she is today, largely influenced by her parents. This resonates with all of us, as we can reflect on our own childhoods and how they shaped our lives, whether the memories are good, bad, or indifferent.

I can't make this stuff up! It's a song that resonates with me and my family history, how my great-grandfather built a foundation of faith that's deep and wide. It's evident in not only my character and personality but in many of my relatives on both sides of my family. The roots of that foundation provide stability both spiritually and mentally, in how I view and approach all that life offers.

Because of what my parents have taught and passed down to me, I am driven as best I can to do the same or better for my kids. One week after my dad passed, I found myself in the master bathroom of his bedroom, getting dressed for his celebration of life service. I noticed some of his jewelry sitting on the bathroom counter. As I was putting on his old watch on one wrist, and his bracelet on the other, my son walked up behind me. He noticed me doing this and asked, "Do you miss your dad?"

Looking at him through the mirror, as he stood behind me, I responded with a firm voice. "Devin, he's only been gone a week so I can't honestly say that I miss him yet, but what I will say is that I will do my best to give you everything he has given to me." I wasn't talking about the watch or the bracelet. I was speaking of the introduction to God, the teaching of His Word, and the countless experiences with my dad that put a smile on my face, and continue to put a smile on my face today, even as I am writing this.

He, for sure, set me up for success, as well as my brothers. We are still benefiting from those lessons taught and learned and will continue to until the day we meet him in heaven. One thing to note: the depth of my spiritual foundation he introduced me to, and sitting in the pews of my grandfather's church, assisted me tremendously through such a difficult time in losing someone so close, but yet knowing he's not far away and this life is not the end. There is so much more to do with him and it will be everlasting. Setting up the proper foundation and having a strong core will give you balance in your life and a level of peace that will serve you, your loved ones, and your co-workers well in the most challenging times of your life.

How would you describe the balance in your life? _____

_____

_____

_____

_____

_____

_____

_____

_____

_____

_____

_____

_____

How do you personally define and perceive balance in your life? _____

_____

_____

_____

_____

_____

What factors or situations make you feel out of balance? ___

_____

_____

_____

_____

_____

_____

_____

What steps do you take to restore balance when it's disrupted?

_____

_____

_____

_____

_____

_____

THE SET UP

Are You Aligned Properly With Your Target?

"Trust in the Lord with all your heart, and do not lean on your own understanding. In all ways acknowledge him, and he will make straight your paths. Be not wise in your own eyes, fear the Lord, and turn away from evil."
—Proverbs 3: 5-7

As I write this chapter, the Master's at Augusta National is only a week away. As I think about Amen Corner, specifically the 11th hole, a par 4 stretching 455 yards with a dogleg to the left, I can't help but think about Ben Hogan's quote, "If you ever see me on the green in two after my second shot on this hole, you'll know I have missed my shot!" Hilarious!

On that hole, there is a body of water that runs along the entire left side of the green. Any ball hit to the left of the green is gone, including shots landing on the slope just off the green, as well as certain areas on the green where the slope is severe enough from right to left for the ball will continue to roll into the water. Ben knew there was a significant risk with aiming for the center of the green and taking a chance of missing it to the left, resulting in a penalty stroke. Therefore, he adopted a more conservative approach by aiming to the right of the green.

Alignment with your target is a "must" and should serve as a guiding principle, still yielding a positive result if missed. Target and alignment are crucial aspects of golf in every shot, and the outcome of the shot heavily depends on these components, to the extent of your capability and accuracy.

Recalling Proverbs 3: 5-7, God is simply asking you to acknowledge Him in all your ways, and He will make your paths straight. Listen to God or seek His counsel for direction in both significant and minor decisions. That one additional component, which is acknowledging God in all the things you set out to do, will eventually align you and set you on a direct course toward your target. Trust and patience are required in this process, as well as seeking His wisdom over your own. Fear God and turn away from evil.

You don't need to devise a complex strategy like the calculations Ben had in his mind during the Master's tournament that year—including his club selection and a target point in another location—to score well on a hole protected by water. Simply ask God for clarity or direction regarding what's on your heart or mind. A sense of peace will accompany those moves led by God.

A dear friend of mine shared with me on multiple occasions that what you feel, think, say, and do should all be congruent. This a good example of alignment in your heart, mind, and soul in your conversations or in activities. As simple as it seems to do just that, add people to the mix who bring in different points of view and beliefs. It becomes a bit more of a challenge.

I also conducted a Google search on alignment in life, and here is what I learned: Alignment is when our thoughts, life choices, and direction all align with our core values. Alignment occurs when we listen to our intuition and move through the world as our true selves. Alignment is the seamless function and action. In my opinion, this concept resonates with what I've learned over the years: to be authentically true to who you are and what you stand for and believe in . This approach greatly assists in living out your passion and purpose without second-guessing yourself. You must be intentional both on the course in relation to your target and off the course in personal activities.

Sometimes we may be unaware. In golf, quite often one may find themselves with a good posture, feet correctly set apart—perhaps shoulder-width—and all the other key attributes of a proper stance, except for their alignment toward the target. This is clearly a result of being unaware or having a misperception of one's alignment while standing over their golf ball. This happens particularly with amateur golfers, perhaps due to a lack of instruction or lessons, or other reasons.

As a result, a golfer may strike the ball well, but find they've missed their target, whether hitting a fairway from the tee or aiming for the green from the fairway toward the pin. This can be frustrating, especially when you had a great swing and hit the ball perfectly. It might end in a penalty stroke due to a hazard the ball lands in, or perhaps a lost ball due to trees or other hazards on the golf course. This is clearly a blind spot the amateur golfer has in their set-up.

One way of resolving this mis-alignment issue in golf is to use two alignment sticks when practicing on the golf range. These alignment sticks are typically thin and lightweight used by golfers to improve their alignment, aim, and swing mechanics. A golfer will place the sticks parallel to the target line to ensure the golfer's feet, hips, and shoulders are properly aligned with their target. Positioning the sticks on the ground to help visualize and practice the correct path of the golf club during the swing. Alignment sticks truly assist the golfer in getting them aligned.

More often than not over the years during a golf round, my friends or fellow golfers golfing with me have straightened me out towards my target because I simply was unaware that

I was misaligned. Grateful for those moments over the years for sure.

I'm also grateful to have been corrected many times over the course of my life when my actions or behavior didn't align with my intentions. Having a lack of clarity may cloud my thoughts about my goals and objectives. Inconsistent actions can be the result of thoughts not aligned with my goals. As a result, I may start and stop projects, change strategies, or engage in behaviors that are counterproductive.

Lastly, when thoughts and actions are at odds with your desired outcome, you may experience stress and anxiety. This emotional discomfort can further hinder your ability to focus and make progress. Though it may feel embarrassing at times, recognizing and understanding the situation early on can be refreshing, preventing you from heading toward an unfavorable outcome.

I'll say it again, trust and lean on God's wisdom and not our own understanding. He will make your paths straight. He will get you aligned and use people and experiences to aid in this effort. A relief indeed!

At times, our actions or communication are not aligned with our beliefs. Our focus can be skewed due to the unconsciousness or unawareness of our belief system caused by outside influences, people with different perspectives, backgrounds, and experiences. The activity we're engaged in or our response to someone may not align with our morals and values. This can lead to discomfort for both ourselves and the person we're addressing. It's important to consider how your words or actions, or the lack thereof, could impact others and alter the outcome of your intent or desire. Your thoughts, feelings, words, and actions should all be congruent. If any of these things are misaligned, several potential negative outcomes may manifest in their respective areas. Alignment is crucial in anything you do and is essential for progressing towards your goals.

In golf, the same principle applies. Your thoughts, the sensation of the club in your hand, your visualization of the golf shot, and your commitment to the swing must all be aligned during setup and target alignment before starting the swing.

Visualize your target. Imagine yourself in that place as if that goal has been achieved. As Lewis Carroll, an English author of *Alice in Wonderland* stated, "If you don't know where you're going, any road will take you there." Maintaining positive thoughts and envisioning yourself experiencing the desired outcome is just as critical as the action itself when aligning your mindset with your goals.

I remember my college days playing for a Division 1 football team in Texas. During pre-game activities, we would warm up on the field to familiarize ourselves with the stadium, especially when playing in unfamiliar venues. Before each game, I would wear a headset with uplifting music, often gospel tunes. At some point during my warm-up, I would visit both end zones on the football field and visualize scenarios like running into the end zone with the ball or catching a pass there. Before a game against Grambling State University in the Cotton Bowl Classic held in Dallas, Texas, my Offensive Coordinator asked me why I was walking around in the end zone. I replied, "I might as well get acquainted with this area since I plan on being here during the game." As it turned out, I scored a touchdown that night. I often employed this practice throughout my college years, and it contributed to my earning the Most Valuable Player award during my junior year after an impressive season.

Imagine if this mindset were incorporated into your daily morning routine before starting your day. Whether you're preparing for school, work, or spending time with family and friends, setting your mind, body, and soul for the day's challenges can be transformative.

Being joyful, grateful, and hopeful while considering the day's agenda, filled with various activities, both work-related and personal, sets a positive tone. As a man of faith, I follow a prescribed set of morning activities to clothe myself with the full armor of God: shoes of peace, belt of truth, breastplate of righteousness, and helmet of salvation. It's undoubtedly one of the most peaceful moments of my day.

Expressing gratitude to God and acknowledging the blessings in your life helps put experiences into perspective.

It's truly an honor to be where I am, enjoying blessings like my health, my wife, my kids, and loved ones. To simply be breathing is a blessing and quite often I take it for granted.

Reading enriching books, incorporating exercise, and listening to preferred music or podcasts could be part of your morning routine. All these activities help me to orient myself towards what I desire for my life. Simply aligning your activities for the day can make a big difference in having a productive day, as it aligns with your target and vision. It works!

What do you want or need to be aligned with in your life right now? _____

_____

_____

_____

_____

_____

_____

_____

_____

What adjustments must you make, if any to ensure you're on the straightest path to your goal? _____

_____

_____

_____

_____

_____

_____

_____

_____

What are your alignment sticks or measures you will incorporate into your life to ensure you stay on the correct path? _____

_____

_____

_____

_____

_____

_____

_____

THE SET UP

Is Your Grip Right?

"So do not fear, for I am with you; do not be dismayed, for I am your God. I will strengthen you and help you; I will uphold you with my righteous right hand."
—Isaiah 41:10

"If it takes me a hundred regrips, it's all right—I'm not going to hit a shot until I'm ready. If it annoys you, don't look until you hear the click." Sergio Garcia, one of the best Professional Golf Association players, shared this advice with reporters in Maui after winning the Mercedes Golf Championship. This victory came after four rounds and an aggregate of more than four thousand fidgety, finicky, seemingly compulsive regrippings of his golf grip. Unfortunately, Sergio gained notoriety for spending an excessive amount of time repeatedly gripping and regripping his club.

Gripping a club refers to the act of holding the club in your hands in preparation for a golf shot. Additionally, there are also three ways—or strengths—in which a golfer can position their fingers in relation to the grip of the club itself—neutral, weak, and strong. A solid grip on the golf club to a golfer can be likened to a security blanket for a toddler. It's something that matters significantly to most golfers as it provides a sense of security before initiating a swing. There are various methods of gripping, such as overlap, interlock, and baseball.

As Christians, there are times when we might feel we have a weak grip on our relationship with God, struggling with the closeness we desire. We might feel we don't quite have a grip on God and His Word. It could be simply how often we are relating with God or the quality of the time we spend with Him.

Life's busyness can easily distract us, leaving us preoccupied with work, family, kids, or school. Our perception of our relationship with God could be likened to the various golf grips: neutral, weak, or strong, depending on the season of life we find ourselves in. I have certainly experienced moments like Sergio's—yearning for a deeper closeness with God, or feeling anxious or nervous before a big presentation, or upon receiving shocking news of a loved one falling ill or passing away. There are numerous situations that can trigger such feelings.

Nonetheless, it brings comfort to remember a scripture in times of unease, Philippians 4:6-7, which states, *"Be anxious for nothing, but in everything by prayer and supplication, with thanksgiving, let your requests be made known to God, and the peace of God, which surpasses all understanding, will guard your hearts and minds through Christ Jesus."* This verse offers so much peace as I truly believe He is with me and can hear and will answer all of my requests. Knowing this instills a calmness in me.

My great friend and mentor, Don Johnson, shared a story with me of a family consisting of a husband, wife, and two daughters. One Saturday morning, while at home, the mother was preparing breakfast. She asked the girls to go upstairs and wake up their father to let him know that breakfast was ready. Naturally, the two sisters engaged in a friendly competition, racing each other upstairs to their parents' bedroom. The youngest daughter had earned the nickname "Postscript" because of her tendency to be a bit slower, as if she were as slow as mail being delivered to someone's home.

As expected, the oldest daughter reached their father's bedside first and hugged him, delivering the message as their mother had instructed. Seconds later, Postscript arrived at the foot of the bed, only to find her big sister already hugging their father and declaring, "No need to tell Daddy. I've already told him breakfast is ready!" To make matters worse, the older sister playfully stuck her tongue out.

In response, Postscript started to cry, a tear escaping from one of her eyes. Recognizing the dynamics at play between the two girls, their father looked at Postscript and warmly requested, "Postscript, come here and lay next to Daddy." He pulled her close under his opposite arm, offering comfort and reassurance. Postscript then glanced across her father's chest, making eye contact with the older sister, and says, "You may have all of Daddy, but Daddy has all of me!"

Anytime you feel like you don't have a good grip on God, He certainly always has a good grip on you. No matter what, He will always be there for you. He will hold you and keep you. He will carry you as much as you need Him to. He will never leave nor forsake you.

There were two moments in my golf career, now spanning over twenty-five years, where I struggled with maintaining a good grip on my golf clubs. The first incident occurred during my first ever round of golf one summer after after graduating from college. It was a day when one of my closest friends, Mickey Washington, an NFL player at the time, invited me for a round of golf.

Here I was, standing on the tee box with a group of NFL players, some of whom were Mickey's teammates. I had a driver in my hand, and all eyes were on me. In this nerve-wracking moment, I realized I had forgotten to put on a golf glove, and I was in Houston, Texas, one of the most humid places on the planet. Despite the pressure, I swung the club as hard as I could, made solid contact, and the ball soared a remarkable distance down the middle of the fairway. The guys were in awe as they watched the ball fly through the air.

While they marveled at the impressive shot, I found myself sprinting to the left side of the fairway, about 100 yards from the tee box, chasing my driver which had also taken flight. It was hilarious! Clearly, I didn't quite have a proper grip on the club that day. A similar incident happened again in Houston a few years later, this time at Tour 18 golf course.

On this occasion, I was using my 3 wood for a tee shot on an elevated tee box of a par 4 hole. After striking the ball, my 3 wood slipped out of my hands mid-swing and landed on a hard, paved cart path, damaging the head of the club about a 100 yards away. That sucked donuts as it was a new club!

Rain, storms, and humidity can undoubtedly affect your grip on your golf club. Similarly, in life, there are trials, tribulations, and challenges that can influence your perspective and the way you connect with God. It's inevitable you will face challenges in your life. The good news is that God will be holding on to you. I'm confident in this because He declared in Isaiah 41:10, "*So do not fear, for I am with you; do not be dismayed, for I am your God. I will strengthen you and help you; I will uphold you with my righteous right hand.*" His grip won't slip regardless of the rain, the humidity, or any other elements or storms that may come your way. No matter what, He will hold us steadfastly.

I clung to this verse for months after my dad's passing. It comforted me and served as a form of therapy, keeping me encouraged. There is no need to regrip because He has a secure grip on you! Furthermore, if you have a good grip on God, you will have a good grip on life!

How is your grip with God at the moment, weak, neutral, or strong? Think of it this way, is your spiritual connection with God currently steady, in need of strengthening, or flourishing?

_____

_____

_____

What meaningful steps can you take to strengthen your grip and/or maintain your connection with Him? _____

_____

_____

_____

As you contemplate your life, recall moments when God demonstrated His unwavering grip on you and list one or two of those here. _____

_____

_____

_____

TRUST

Trust Your Swing

"But blessed is the one who trusts in the Lord, whose confidence is in him. They will be like a tree planted by the water that sends out its roots by the stream. It does not fear when heat comes, its leaves are always green. It has no worries in a year of drought and never fails to bear fruit."
—Jeremiah 17: 7-8

Trust is an assured reliance on the character, ability, strength, or truth of someone or something, a foundation on which confidence is built. It involves a dependence on something future or contingent, akin to hope. Synonyms for trust include faith and confidence. After the golfer has taken their stance and positioned themselves with a solid foundation, a momentary pause, lasting a split second or possibly longer occurs between the initial setup and the subsequent pullback of the golf club, followed by the forward motion to strike the golf ball. Within this fleeting instant, a crucial determinant of whether the swing will be successful or not is the level of trust in the golfer's swing coach, instructional videos, golf articles, personal abilities, and ultimately the belief in their own capacity to execute the shot.

The phase of trust is just as important for a golfer on the putting surface, with the putter in hand, as they assess factors like the greens' angulation, speed, direction of the blades of grass, and the length of the grass. Either way, this is the time when trusting your swing becomes paramount. This trust might have been built during practice sessions prior to the round, through golf lessons from a local pro, or even from a short instructional video you've watched. Regardless of the source, it's time to press the "go" button.

How you trust, the depth of that trust in yourself, and even whom you trust will significantly influence a golfer's swing experience. Over the following four chapters, we will delve into four key critical considerations for this trust phase in golf. We will explore how the concept manifests in your swing, your caddie, your mental strength, and the relationship between your mind, body, and soul, and how this trust can govern your actions and shape their outcomes.

There are numerous types of golf swings. While it can be argued that no two are exactly alike from start to finish, many swing styles on the PGA Tour exhibit remarkable similarities. However, there are poor and unique swings that are sometimes hard to watch, while others are unorthodox and quite interesting but work well, such as Jim Furyk's swing. The most crucial factor leading to positive outcomes in any of these swings is consistency. The more consistent, the more you trust it. Confidence rises, and stress diminishes. You own your swing! Consistent golf swings typically lead to success in tournaments, much like in other sports where skill mastery is crucial for achieving victories.

Regardless of the type of swing, the same key component that plays heavily into the quality of the swing is trust. A golfer must have unwavering trust in themselves and their abilities when standing over a golf ball. Full trust in their swing is imperative before initiating the club's backward motion. Without it, the desired outcome could be compromised. This concept extends beyond golf to everyday life. God has crafted humans with the inherent need to trust nearly every thought and action. Even as you read or listen to this book, the level of trust in its content determines how much you retain and take action to apply it.

As I contemplate a golfer's trust in their swing and the ultimate goal of successful performance, I also reflect on how God has endowed each of us with physical and spiritual gifts. I bring this up because I want you to recognize, embrace, and have confidence in both your innate talents and any acquired skills you possess. The greater your self-awareness and confidence in wielding these abilities, the more success and inner peace you'll achieve when putting them into practice. When we trust ourselves, we typically think and act more swiftly, both mentally and physically, compared to when we lack self-assurance. Speed can be a valuable indicator for assessing trust levels. That's why I've linked it to a crucial moment when you start moving your body to swing a golf club. Depending on the task at hand you are involved in, speed in this manner will make the difference in a major way. And for the record, and a side note, your God-given gifts serve a purpose and exist solely for His pleasure. Colossians 1:16 affirms that all things were created by Him and for Him. Our purpose, formed in God's image, is to know, love, worship, serve, and fellowship with Him. This requires trust in both God as the Designer and ourselves. Trust yourself, trust God and the gifts you have!

Discovering our innate talents can be effortless for most. It's something done well without conscious effort. Alternatively, it could relate to our physical attributes. Without delving into specifics, it's essential to identify our gifts and discern if and when God intends for us to use them. Knowing our purpose and use of our gifts may occur early or late in life. Be confident in this: *"He who began a good work in you will complete it until the day of Christ Jesus,"* Philippians 1:6. Trust in this verse, written by Paul and inspired by God. Paul encourages confidence not only in our perseverance but also in our sanctification—the process of becoming Christ-like. We must seek to grow in our faith and not wait until the end of our lives. Trust in our abilities to accomplish meaningful work for God and others, be it at home, on the job, on the golf course, or anywhere else.

For we are God's masterpiece, created in Christ Jesus to do good works that He prepared in advance for us to do (Ephesians 2:10). This embodies the essence of trust and influences the human spirit, driving how we live. For instance, trusting your instincts or trusting your gut—how often have you had that experience? Did you act on them?

In golf, trust can shape a golf swing when it comes to the accuracy of the swing plane and speed. We touched on speed earlier and how it can impact our thoughts and actions across various aspects of our activities. Let's think about this for a minute more specifically related to golf. The speed of your swing, in essence, could be a reflection of your confidence or trust. In golf, deceleration is a bad thing, and this typically occurs when one loses confidence or trust in their swing during the actual downswing. As a result, an errant shot occurs, and it's costly. How can trust change the outcomes of your performance at the job, in your marriage, your relationships, or in your health? How can trust change or steer the desired outcomes in these areas of your life?

Trust in the business, as it pertains to leadership's vision and strategy that result in initiatives requiring you to do something different. The desire and speed at which you trust those initiatives or in your leadership vary. Trust in your spouse has a huge impact on the marriage. Trust or the lack thereof can likely affect the quality of your sleep. Trust plays a significant role in your health influencing your confidence in the food you consume and ultimately shaping your reliance on the advice provided by your family doctor.

I recall many conversations with my doctor, Dr. Felix Horng, where I've valued and taken his advice. He has proven to be credible, reliable, and trustworthy, supported by the credentials, including the fourteen years I've been seeing him since I arrived here in Orange County, California. My speedy responses to his recommendations, whether prescriptions or diet, due to trust, I'm sure has resulted in success of prevention of illnesses.

There are many countless examples of how trust is used daily in every aspect of our lives. It's imperative to get a handle on it as it defines who you are and who you will become and even perhaps how long you will be here on Earth.

Trusting in God brings about comfort and cheer, even in the midst of stress and difficulties. Faith is what helps us trust God in those difficult times. Difficult times comes in all shapes and sizes. Sometimes, it isn't a drastic tragedy but can be the busy chaos of managing life. Trust is a significant influence in your life, manifesting in various aspects of your existence. It serves as a crucial element. Relying on God to navigate challenges can instill a sense of peace not only for that specific issue but also for others as the day unfolds.

Jeremiah 32:27, *"Behold, I am the Lord, the God of all flesh. Is anything too hard for me?"* God was speaking to Jeremiah. Israel has once again disobeyed God, and they are going to be taken by the Babylonians into captivity for a long period of time. However, God would eventually save His people from the hands of the Babylonians. He will surely save, protect, and help us through our most difficult times. We just have to trust Him.

Reflect on your accomplishments and moments when you excelled. Note those here to better understand your strengths and talents. _____

_____

_____

_____

_____

_____

_____

_____

_____

_____

_____

Replace self-doubt with positive self-talk. Challenge your negative thoughts and replace them with affirmations that reinforce your confidence in your talents. _____

_____

_____

_____

_____

_____

_____

_____

_____

_____

What areas in your life do you need to trust yourself, and God for more? Write your prayer request to God below. ___

_____

_____

_____

_____

_____

_____

_____

_____

TRUST

Who's Your Caddie?

"Where there is no counsel, the people will fall;
but in the multitude of counselors there is safety."
—Proverbs 11:14

One of the best golfer-caddie relationships I've ever heard of was between Tom Watson and Bruce Edwards. Tom Watson was a PGA golfer for years and won numerous tournaments, including a couple of major tournaments like The Masters twice. Bruce Edwards was his caddie for over thirty years. Their caddie-friendship was evident, and each were not shy about expressing it.

Tom shared a story from one round where he followed his usual pre-shot routine with Bruce. On this particular day, as they stood in the fairway of Olympia Fields Country Club at the 2003 U.S. Open, Tom positioned himself next to his golf bag as he usually does, his ball laying on the fairway, while Bruce performed his routine calculations to get the distance to the pin on the green. It's likely Bruce considered factors such as wind and the green's angulation to determine the distance.

After Tom noticed Bruce finished measuring the yardage, he posed the typical question that golfers often ask their caddies—inquiring about the distance to the hole.

Bruce responded, albeit in a voice difficult for Tom to interpret, "A yardage."

Tom, known for his close bond with Bruce, demonstrated incredible patience and understanding. He leaned in close to Bruce and said, "Bruce, I can't understand you, but I know you're trying your best."

Unfortunately, what just happened was the inevitable outcome that both Tom and Bruce knew would come one day. Bruce was transitioning into the next phase of ALS— Amyotrophic Lateral Sclerosis, also known as Lou Gehrig's disease. It's a condition in which a person, while maintaining their mental faculties, loses the ability to walk, talk, and eventually breathe.

The beauty of this story lies in the amazing caddie-friend relationship and partnership both Tom and Bruce exemplified on the PGA Tour. This was a poignant moment that showcased their deep friendship and resilience of the human spirit in the face of adversity. Tom Watson and Bruce Edward's relationship was celebrated for its enduring strength and support, even in the midst of such a challenging circumstance. If you watch golf, you'll find many golfer-caddie stories that showcase true friendships that last a lifetime in golf and in their personal lives. It's a partnership where both individuals uplift each other both on and off the course.

We all need a good caddie like Bruce was to Tom in our lives. We may call them mentors, friends, life coaches, professional coaches, leaders, and so on. These individuals are the ones we can rely on to provide the best advice that will help you make decisions, offer motivation, inspire you, and assist in many other ways.

As much as I believe that all these different types of people are important and a "must have" on our personal board of directors, I would not, for one minute, exclude the advice of the Holy Spirit of God. He's always available twenty-four hours a day, seven days a week, and will listen and speak to you about all things. He is an expert in every industry, resides in your heart, and serves as a guide and a counselor. The Holy Spirit is the third of the Trinity in Christianity: God, Jesus, and the Holy Spirit. He dwells inside of every true believer and is a constant companion on the walk of faith. He is all-loving, forgiving, merciful and just. Unlike a human caddie, for a golfer who may make mistakes at times when calling the correct yardage based on wind, rain, and other elements, the Holy Spirit makes no mistakes as He is perfect. Our challenge as humans is to listen and obey Him.

John 14:26 makes it plain: *"But the Advocate, the Holy Spirit, whom the Father will send in my name, will teach you all things and will remind you of everything I have said to you."*

The Holy Spirit will remind you of those commandments and scriptures you have read that could be helpful when needed. Listening to the Holy Spirit will lead to the joy of living a Spirit-led life!

God recommends that we have a caddie, a friend to accompany us through life. No one can go through life alone. It's a wonderful thing to have counsel, someone with whom you can talk to and who will listen to you about anything and everything without fear of judgment or criticism. You need someone you trust, someone who will create a safe and warm environment for you. As John C. Maxwell, an American author, speaker, and pastor who has written many leadership books, states, "Your advisors can make or break you."

Proverbs 11:14 says, *"Where there is no counsel, the people will fall; but in the multitude of counselors, there is safety."* Therefore, everyone needs a personal board of directors, individuals in their circle of friends who will add value to their lives. Once again, John lays it out very well:

- Creative people
- Loyal people
- People who share your vision
- Wise and intelligent people
- People with complimentary gifts
- People with influence
- People of faith
- People of integrity

These are great characteristics that John has recommended, and they provide a great starting point for identifying those people in your life who will guide you in the right direction and help utilize the talents and gifts that God has given you. These individuals will encourage and uplift you. As the saying goes, "iron sharpens iron," meaning individuals will improve each other through constructive challenges and interactions much like iron tools becoming sharper when they rub against one another.

Even in golf, it's priceless when you meet new people and have the opportunity to spend over four hours chatting about various topics. These conversations can often provide exactly the answers you may have been seeking but didn't have. They might open doors in your business or simply offer a listening ear and advice that you need.

USGA President Fred Perpall articulated this sentiment well: "We talk too much about what separates us, and not enough about what unites us. In golf, we're a community. When we lean in together, when we include more people in the game, not only will the game get better, but our lives will get better too." This is, indeed, a profound statement worth hearing and encouraging, to say the least.

A good caddie can make a significant difference for a PGA golfer and certainly enhance the experience of an amateur golfer on any given day. With the Holy Spirit's guidance, He is always with me, whether I'm entering board room meetings or spending time with family and friends. Following His advice will always lead to the right path and bring success in those respective areas of your life.

How about relationships that you've established? How did you go about building them? What key steps did you take to solidify these relationships, especially if that was your intent? I frequently suggest to individuals that cultivating a network of relationships, essentially forming a board of directors, can be beneficial. These are individuals you can trust. This is particularly important for holding yourself accountable in achieving desired success in areas such as spiritual, physical, emotional, relational, and financial health.

This network can help align your direction with your values, ethics, desires, or goals. In a business context, it's wise to seek advice from an impartial and trustworthy source with a demonstrated history of ethical conduct, particularly one who has found success in your industry.

Alternatively, consider your family doctor, to whom you trust and possesses personal characteristics to which you can relate. This doctor can provide a comfortable space for you to express any health concerns you may have regarding your body. I mentioned earlier Dr. Felix Horng, who has been both a great friend and doctor, helping me in many ways over the years. In fact, we see each other once a year for my annual physical, sometimes even twice a year, depending on the circumstances. Dr. Horng offers advice based on my overall health and an evaluation of the basic functions of my organs, updates any vaccinations, and helps me maintain good health.

Again, a personal board of directors should be thoughtfully chosen or established in your life as a means of providing advice or simply being a trusted source with a positive influence in those key areas of your life as mentioned earlier: spiritual, physical, emotional, relational, and financial health.

Humans are naturally inclined to form relationships, and the benefits of these connections are often significant and rewarding. There's a saying, "Show me a person's mentor or peer group, and I'll show you who that person will become." I've also heard someone say that you are the average of those people in your closest network of friends, whether it's three of five people. The key takeaway here is to establish depth in your personal board of directors.

Personally, I have friends whom I've entrusted with the task of providing physical accountability. They are my workout partners, like Morgan Trent, former NFL football player, but more importantly one of my personal board members, who keeps me accountable physically and in my faith. He meets me first thing in the morning, whether five-thirty or six, to kick-start my day at the gym.

Over several days a week, I've reaped the benefits of consistency in the gym and in the pool, thanks to Morgan, who motivates me to not only show up for the workouts but also to push myself and complete them. The return on investment is priceless: great health, no pain, few illnesses like colds or flu, and an abundance of energy to devote to my wife and kids after long hours of work.

My confidence is high, my self-esteem is robust, and my outlook on life is optimistic. These workouts have truly prepared my body and health to endure and sustain energy through some of life's most challenging days. I highly recommend it.

How about in the spiritual aspect of life? How can establishing a strong spiritual foundation set you up for success, and what does this foundation look like?

For me, it involves spending time reading my Bible daily and delving into a God's truths and promises for me. I start my day by thanking God for all He has provided and done for me.

I meditate on His Word, reflecting on what it means for my life and any challenges I may be currently facing. I ask God for strength, healing, and wisdom to navigate decisions, whether in my personal life or at work.

Consistently spending time with Him through reading and studying the Bible helps me recall scriptures that are relevant when I face difficult challenges or experience moments of His goodness. It also includes studying the Bible with members of my personal board of directors, such as Tony Jonas, Lynn Stone, and Jeff Shetler.

Additionally, for the past ten years, I have been a part of a monthly Bible study with some of my closest friends, family members, and others across the country. These are additional personal board members who provide spiritual and uplifting counsel to assist me in overcoming any dark hours and adversity I find myself in.

And lastly, one of my strongest and longest-standing members of my personal board is a specialist in multiple areas. At a minimum, she listens to all propositions and issues I encounter. She is almost always available, and when she isn't, she gets back to me as soon as she is available. Known as my confidant, my rock, and frankly, my all, she is my wife, Demetris. We have been personal and professional partners for twenty-nine years. I can confide in her, and she provides a safe, nonjudgmental, warm, and loving place on which I can depend. I married her twenty-five years ago because of her commitment to me, her consistency in who she is, the passion and chemistry we share, and, more importantly, because of her faith in God.

Allow me to remind you that when any of these individuals I mention is unavailable for to me for some reason or another due to their innate human nature, I always can depend on the Holy Spirit and God's Word for counsel. He is my #1 caddie! He's the CEO of my personal board of directors. My faith is the most critical part of my being, and I try to incorporate as much learning from God's Word as possible into my schedule to keep me grounded, centered, and prepared for any "course" in life. By "course," I mean life experiences that equip me to teach others. These experiences draw me closer to God and His scripture, where I learn how to reflect on these experiences and use them to glorify God through ministry to others.

As 2 Timothy 3:15 states, "All scripture is God-breathed and is useful for teaching, rebuking, correcting, and training in righteousness, so that the servant of God may be thoroughly equipped for every good work." I posed the question at the beginning of this chapter: "Who is your caddie?"

Who's your caddie? _____

_____

_____

Which individuals make up your personal board of directors? Please list those individuals below and express to them the meaningful roles they hold in your life. _____

_____

_____

Do you think there's a need to include new members on your personal board or possibly remove some existing ones? _____

_____

_____

TRUST

It's A Mental Game

"Do not conform to the pattern of this world, but be transformed by the renewing of your mind. Then you will be able to test and approve what God's will is—His good, pleasing and perfect will."
—Romans 12:2

"So shall a man thinketh, so shall he be," Proverbs 23:7. I remember my early teens when I visited my uncle Harvey in the Bay Area. He was an avid golfer, and at that time, I hadn't even considered taking up the game of golf then. We were watching a PGA Tour event on television, engaged in conversations about golf and life. During the broadcast, a golfer was preparing to hit his shot from the fairway, aiming for a green surrounded by water on three of its four sides. To me, it looked to be an extremely tough shot, and the commentator expressed similar concerns, mentioning that the golfer could easily find his ball in the lake with even the slightest mistake. In response, I made a statement to my uncle, exclaiming, "Look at all that water around that green!" My uncle's response was both humorous and enlightening as he said, "What water?" I burst into laughter but never forgot such a valuable lesson he taught me: "You are who you think you are."

Indeed, the mind holds immense power, often stronger than the body in many ways. It's about confidence and perspective—whether you see the glass as half-full or half-empty. In golf, the mental aspect plays a pivotal role. The game of golf is predominantly a mental challenge, with the mental component outweighing the physical one for avid golfers, especially professionals. In golf, your decisions, thoughts, mental images, and feelings shape each swing. Mental training helps players develop essential mental skills to complement the mechanics or physical aspects of their game. Golfers who perform in the zone exhibit composure, control, confidence, and unwavering focus.

In an article by Patrick Cohn and Michael Edgar on the mental game of golf, the authors highlighted specific attributes a golfer must possess to be mentally tough:

1) Having an awareness of the zone, and the feelings associated with playing in the zone.
2) High self-confidence or a strong belief in their skills or ability to play well.
3) The ability to be fully immersed in the task or totally concentrate in the present.

4) A narrow focus of attention or the ability to concentrate on one specific thought without distraction.

5) The ability to swing effortlessly or let it happen when it counts.

6) Emotional control or the ability to remain calm under pressure.

7) A clear and decisive mind, avoiding overthinking and self-doubt.

8) The ability to refocus or collect themselves after mistakes or making a bad shot.

9) Finding enjoyment in the game, whether they are 10 over par or 2 under par.

A strong mental game is crucial for all golfers, and a strong spiritual game holds true for all humans! Let's adapt the principles mentioned above from golfers to humans living on Earth:

1) *"Do you know that your body is a temple of the Holy Spirit who dwells within you, whom you have from God, and that you are not your own?"* (1 Corinthians 6:19)

2) *"I can do all things through Him who strengthens me."* (Philippians 4:13)

3) *"Therefore, do not worry about tomorrow, for tomorrow will worry about itself. Each day has enough trouble of its own."* (Matthew 6:34)

4) In Matthew 14:29-30, *"Peter got out of the boat, walked on water, and came to Jesus."*

5) *"Cast all your worries and cares upon God, for He cares for you."* (1 Peter 5:7)

6) *"Don't worry about anything; instead, pray about everything. Tell God what you need, and thank Him for all He has done. Then you will experience God's peace, which surpasses anything we can understand."* (Philippians 4:6-7)

7) *"Be strong and courageous. Do not be afraid; do not be discouraged, for the Lord your God is with you wherever you go."* (Joshua 1:9)

8) *"Remember not the former things, nor consider the things of old. Behold, I am doing a new thing; now it springs forth. Do you not perceive it?"* (Isaiah 43:18-19)

9) *"And we know that in all things God works for the good of those who love Him, who have been called according to His purpose."* (Romans 8:29)

Just as golf is a mental game, life is a spiritual warfare. We must always be alert and engaged, continuously preparing our minds, renewing our spirits, and living lives that are pleasing and acceptable to God. There will be many trials and tribulations, along with temptations and distractions along the way. However, we must not give in to those traps that can easily beset us and divert us from focusing on what God tends to accomplish within us, upon us, and through us. It's a daily task that can only be managed one day at a time.

In the fall of 2018, my brother-in-law, Robert Holden and his family were visiting us from Texas. It was a great time spent with them, barbecuing, golfing, and watching my oldest, Devin, play high school basketball. One night after his basketball practice, Robert, Devin, and I needed to stop by a cigar lounge in Newport Beach to pick up a few cigars and more propane for his lighter. So, we stopped by a nearby lounge.

As we stepped out of our vehicle, I asked Devin to stay in the car and wait for us while Robert and I approached the front of the store, which was all glass. That's when Robert noticed Dennis Rodman, one of the best NBA defensive players ever, sitting inside the lounge. He stopped me in my tracks, placing his hand on my chest to prevent me from taking one more step, and said, "Kerwin, that's Dennis Rodman!" I looked and agreed. He told me to wait while he went to get Devin out of the car and asked him to come in with us to say hi to Dennis.

As we went into the lounge, Dennis immediately stood up, came towards me with open arms, and gave me a hug. He thought I was Derek Fisher, one of his old teammates, as people have told me throughout my adult years that I favor him. Dennis then hugged my brother-in-law and my son, and there was an exchange of greetings as we continued toward the humidor located towards the back of the lounge. The three of us were amazed and full of excitement to have had the opportunity to see Dennis Rodman and receive such a greeting. However, it gets better!

You see, while the three of us were in the humidor, still tripping over the fact that Dennis was just six 6 feet away outside, having given us such an amazing greeting, I turned to my son, who still had his mouth wide open in awe, and asked him to go out and let Dennis know that he had played against his son for a couple of years in both high school and AAU basketball.

Devin had always been tasked by his coach to help with defending Dennis Rodman, Jr., as he was the best offensive player Devin's team faced every single time their teams played against each other. So, Devin had his fair share of work during those games, but did an exceptional job defending him, as Devin was considered one of the best defenders in basketball at that time. Devin responded with much anxiety and nervousness in his voice that he would do it.

I decided to take ownership and do it myself to spare him some stress. I approached Dennis with my phone and showed him a still photo of Devin driving to the rim with Dennis Rodman Jr. guarding him—a remarkable action shot.

I asked Dennis to take a look at it and inquired, "Who's the guy guarding my son?"

He responded, "That's my son, man!"

I replied, "Yeah, and he's good, too! The two of them go at it like cats and dogs when they're playing against each other! It's been so much fun watching them compete over the years."

Dennis caught me off-guard and asked, "Would you mind if I take your son outside and give him a few basketball tips? It would be my honor and a way of giving back to you for sharing with me photos of my son and the story you shared."

I told him it would not be a problem at all.

We went outside, and Dennis spoke to my son while Robert and I listened for twenty minutes. Dennis was pouring into Devin, telling him that I, as a father, have laid it out for him, and all Devin had to do was pick it up and use it. He also assured Devin that he would be going to the NBA, and when he got there, he would be doing a lot of traveling and staying in hotels. Dennis advised him that every hotel room had a Bible inside, and all Devin needed to do was open the drawer on the nightstand, find the Bible, and read it. "Just open it up," he repeated to Devin, demonstrating with his hands as if he were holding a Bible and flipping it open to read.

After several minutes of Dennis affirming my son and offering encouragement, he turned to me and asked me an astounding request. "Dad, tell me one thing about life!" Well, maybe it wasn't a request, but more of a demand, as if he was searching for something.

Miraculously, I responded like this, "You must die to yourself every day, give yourself to God, get out of your way.

Don't think about the past, nor think about the future. Take it one day at a time. Be present in the moment!"

Dennis responded, "God!"

I responded, "You just told my son about the Bible, so I know you are a man of faith!"

At this point, Dennis began to cry, and I assured him that I would be praying for him and his family.

I had a sense that Dennis was reflecting on his son and their relationship, whether it was good, bad, or indifferent. I do know that God was present in that conversation. Just as in golf, where we must be present in the moment for every shot and not dwell on the previous or upcoming hole, we must also be present in everything we do in life, allowing the Holy Spirit to move and speak through us in all situations. We should take it one day at a time because that's how God designed us, not to take in everything all at once. We shouldn't worry about food, shelter, or anything we may face, as God has it all under control. Our minds should be focused on Him, and He will guide us through and step in from time to time, as He did this night with Dennis, transforming my way of thinking to focus on the eternal rather than the external. I was able to guide and advise Dennis to be present in the moment no different than I was present in the moment as I enjoyed such an amazing encounter with him while with my son and brother-in-law. God gives us exactly what we need, and he did that through me in response to such a simple, but great question Dennis Rodman asked me.

God also provided manna to the Israelites for forty years as they journeyed through the wilderness in order for God to speak to them because of their unwillingness to take the land of Egypt as He directed. It's a beautiful thing! It's a great example of how He takes care of us daily even if we find ourselves in the wilderness. However, stay mentally focused and be prepared at all times to respond to or seize opportunities that may arise in your life.

How's your mental state or mindset? _____

_____

_____

_____

_____

_____

_____

_____

_____

_____

_____

Do you feel that your mind is adequately prepared to deal with any situation that may arise? _____

_____

_____

_____

_____

_____

_____

_____

_____

_____

List the actions you can take to safeguard and enhance your mental well-being. _____

_____

_____

_____

_____

_____

_____

_____

_____

_____

TRUST

Strong Mind, Strong Body, Strong Soul

"Now to Him who is able to do far more abundantly than all that we ask or think, according to the power at work within us, to Him be the glory in the church and in Christ Jesus throughout all generations, forever and ever. Amen."
—Ephesians 3:20

When the mind, body, and soul are synchronized in golf, remain open-minded for the unimaginable to take place if required. You may have seen Tiger's chip shot on the 16th hole, par 3 at the Masters in 2005 when the ball just barely dropped inside the hole, almost sealing the victory with a couple of holes left to play. I've seen other remarkable shots on the tour and, frankly, even in my own golf experiences.

Let's consider experiences, accomplishments, and opportunities in our lives that we have been a part of. Think about projects you may have worked on, activities you've been involved in, or accomplishments that make you most proud. There may have been challenges you have overcome as well. I challenge you to dig deep into your mental archive to acknowledge and celebrate, for a moment, when you have conquered small or large feats.

We discussed the mental aspect of golf in our experiences and how to prepare for great things and great challenges on the course. As we think about having a strong mind, body, and soul in life, I want us to embrace what God has blessed us with, as it states in Ephesians, that He can do far more than we can ask or imagine. It's a matter of whether we trust Him. When faced with difficulty in any area, we can find hope and a burst of energy toward overcoming what may be deemed difficult at the time if we trust Him. It's in our mind. The strength of our mental is truly correlated to our trust in Him and in ourselves.

Typically, it's a rehearsal of seeing it play through in my head repeatedly. I visualize it, pray about it, believe in it, and see it completed to my desire. When officiating weddings, I meticulously practice the words I convey to couples well in advance of the actual event. It gives me confidence and belief that it will go as I envisioned it. It's never perfect, but it comes very close to my desires, and hopefully, in turn, to my clients as well. The mind is as strong as your level of belief in yourself.

In Romans 7:18, Paul says, *"And I know that nothing good lives in me, that is, in my sinful nature. I want to do what is right, but I can't. I want to do what is good, but I don't. I don't want to do what is wrong, but I do it anyway."* What a great way to explain when the mind and body are not connected. Paul, in essence, is saying that your body and mind are always at odds, but only with God's help can you get them synced up more often than not.

Your mind controls your body to an extent, and any doubt will change its direction. Aligning the two requires constant effort, particularly when faced with unimaginable circumsances, as I mentioned earlier. You have to constantly train both, no different than a golfer training muscle memory in their swing mechanics. Repetitions of a God-given talent exercised has the potential to turn into a powerful strength. The more you train your body to do what you desire, the more it becomes inclined to respond accordingly. This process is similar to practicing on the golf range or engaging in exercise to train and condition your body.

Even what we say or speak about to our family, friends, and co-workers has so much to do with what we listen to, what we read, and/or what we see. As a result, be mindful and intentional of how you spend your time. If you're eating unhealthy, then your organs could potentially be damaged and negatively affect your overall health. Vice versa, if you eat healthily and exercise regularly, it will positively affect your overall health. Runners run to train. Golfers hit the range to refine their game. Basketball players shoot, dribble, and practice continuously to improve their skills. Take deliberate action when it comes to your body and the specific goals you're training it to achieve.

As a man of faith, I often read God's Word to put on the full armor of God. I pray and meditate on His Word. In various aspects of my life, I regularly seek help and assistance from God. This prepares my mind for battles I may experience in life. Let's be mindful of the inputs into our minds and bodies through what we hear, see, and do.

The soul is an emotional or intellectual energy or intensity, especially as revealed in a work of art or an artistic performance. Another definition of soul is the spiritual or immaterial part of a human being or animal, regarded as immortal. You may have heard the saying that a person who is performing extremely well exemplifies that their heart and soul was in it, relating to their performance. I like the idea of doing my very best to act and make decisions with my heart and soul in mind, particularly major things. God says, "But if from there you seek the Lord your God, you will find Him if you seek Him with all your heart and with all of your soul," Deuteronomy 4:29. He even gives strong advice as to how to seek Him with all of your heart and soul. That will increase your trust in Him and help you trust yourself when you're putting your soul into something.

Tiger Woods, and many others on the PGA Tour absolutely do this in the game of golf! Other athletes in other sports do this as well. It's their passion, and it shows up very well in sports. To sum up, those who achieve success in their craft have dedicated their entire being, and I would assume that includes their soul.

Here's something worth sharing: my wife, kids, and I have created vision boards over the years, typically during New Year's Eve. We write our dreams on a vision board that encompasses our thoughts, where we see ourselves, and what our souls speak to us.

To make it plain, there are things, including the writing and publishing of this book, that exist on my vision board. I literally drew a bookshelf on my vision board with several of my favorite books, including the Bible. One additional book that I included in that vision board over six years ago was titled *Follow Through*. Now, I am just months away from releasing it to the world.

Trusting our actions will eventually support our dreams. As I've said before, life rewards actions. My prayer is that those actions are in alignment with God's will and direction for my life. He also gives me confidence, as it is written in His Word in Ephesians 2:10, "For we are God's handiwork, created in Christ Jesus to do good works, which God prepared in advance for us to do." This is my life verse. It's already laid out for us. We just have to put our mind, body, and soul into it.

Do you feel that your mind, body, heart, and spirit are aligned and in harmony in everything you undertake? _____

_____

_____

_____

_____

_____

_____

_____

What occasional activities or exercises can you engage in to practice and embody this concept in your daily life? _____

_____

_____

_____

_____

_____

What is your life verse? Write it below. _____

_____

_____

_____

_____

_____

COMMIT

Life Rewards Action—Act in Faith

"But be doers of the word, and not hearers only,
deceiving yourselves."
—James 1:22

"**S**tay committed to the swing!" How many times have you heard this in your golf career? When you don't commit to your swing, the results could be catastrophic. You may not get your body weight transferred, and you might come out of your swing, leaving the slot position during your follow-through. These are just a couple of swing mechanics among several that can lead to shortcomings in a successful golf swing due to a lack of commitment or taking action. Frequently, a golfer engages in self-talk and understands what they should do, but their greatest challenge lies in putting that understanding into action.

During a golf round many years ago, my good friend, Lance Gomes, found himself in the fairway on a par 4 hole approximately 150 yards away from the pin. It was an ideal position. He pulled the club back and took a swing, but to our surprise, the ball shot straight to the right, almost like a shank. For those that are not golfers, a shank is when a golfer hits the ball with intention for it to go straight, and in this case, the ball goes directly ninety degrees to the right of the club immediately if the golfer is a right-hand golfer. It is the worst golf shot in golf. In several cases, a golfer continues to hit all or most of their golf shots in this "shank" fashion as it can be challenging to work their way out of it.

As he placed the club back in his golf bag and walked over to his ball, he couldn't help but blurt out, "You have to go through the checklist, Lance. Go through the checklist!" He knew the right thing to do, but somehow failed to do it. I've been guilty of this as well, and I'm sure at least a few of you have experienced something similar. This situation reminds me of moments in my life, whether in golf, at work, in my relationships, or in my faith, where I knew what was best for me but ended up doing the opposite, something different, or even nothing at all.

I have had a few golf lessons over the course of my golf career. It can be the most difficult thing for me to participate in at times. You often have to unlearn some things before you can grasp onto learning something new that's better for your golf swing. It can be extremely challenging to unlearn things you have been doing for years that have seemed to have worked out okay for you. However, if you want to get better, you have to do the things to get better. By being open to unlearning, you create space to absorb and understand the new concepts and techniques that will ultimately improve your golf swing or whatever your craft or skill set is you're working on. Get rid of the old habits and form new good habits that yield good results.

1 Peter 1:14 says it very well, *"So you must live as God's obedient children."* Don't slip back into your old ways of living to satisfy your own desires.

What keeps us from taking action? Fear? Fear of failure, fear of rejection, or the unknown can paralyze us and prevent us from taking action, even if we know it's the right thing to do. Being in our comfort zone is another challenge. We often resist stepping out of our comfort zones, even when we know that doing so would be beneficial.

There are several other factors, such as procrastination, lack of confidence, external pressures, and more. To overcome these obstacles, it's essential to develop self-awareness and identify the specific barriers holding us back from taking action. Working on building self-confidence, managing fear, setting realistic goals, and seeking support from others can help us take action on the things we know are right to do. I'll discuss more in detail on seeking the support of others later in the book.

Taking action necessitates faith, belief, or trust, along with a strong commitment and willingness to embrace some degree of risk. Action enables us to transform the invisible into the visible. Additionally, embracing a growth mindset and viewing failures as opportunities for learning can empower us to move forward and make positive changes in our lives. In golf, swinging the club demands exertion or physical effort. Indeed, in life, achieving your life goals and aspirations also demands effort and hard work. What's refreshing and fulfilling is that life rewards those who take action.

Of course, I have to mention this: there can be, or likely will be, at some point the temptation to go back to old habits, places, or activities in our lives where it's comfortable, perhaps even an addiction to something or someone. That something that feels good or is a ton of fun, but at the cost of your health or the sacrifice of time spent with your loved ones. But do know that God always provides a way out to go a different direction and to abort. He is faithful and will not let you be tempted beyond your ability, but with the temptation He will also provide the way of escape so that you may be able to endure it (1 Corinthians 10:13).

Taking both points into consideration, acting in faith as doers while shedding old behaviors that may hinder you or lead to undesired results, and simultaneously adopting new behaviors that will contribute to your success is no small feat. It requires effort, faith, and God's help. If you listen to

God's Word and obey, He will bless you for your actions. Your behavior and attitude should reflect your actions rather than just listening. It's a commitment to God and a commitment to yourself. You can observe the effectiveness of taking action versus not taking action. God will reward and bless you throughout your life. *"Don't grow weary of doing good, for at the proper time, you will reap a harvest if you don't give up,"* Galatians 6:9. This principle has practical applications in life. You will receive your rewards at the right time.

Acting in faith means trusting and believing that your actions will yield outcomes that please you and ultimately bless you in the eyes of God. Galatians 6:9 serves as a reminder to persevere in doing good deeds, showing kindness, and living a righteous life, even when we face challenges and discouragement. The promise of reaping a harvest suggests that your efforts in doing good will eventually bear fruit and bring positive outcomes, although the timing may not always be immediate.

Your actions and choices have significance, contributing to God's greater plan for your life. Through your actions, you will glorify God. Faith is not solely a matter of intellectual understanding or listening; it involves living out God's teachings in your thoughts, words, and actions.

What's the ratio between your listening and taking action in your life? _____

_____

_____

_____

_____

_____

_____

_____

_____

_____

_____

How can you enhance your ability to listen and act effectively, thus improving your listening-to-doing ratio? _____

_____

_____

_____

_____

_____

_____

_____

_____

COMMIT

Take Risk—Go For It!

"Where there is no risk, there is no faith!"
—Tim Cooper, Walmart Executive

In the final round of the 2004 Masters, Phil Mickelson was trailing the leader, Ernie Els, by one stroke as he stood on the 18th hole at the Master's Tournament at Augusta National golf course, which is a challenging par 4. Playing it safe would likely lead to a playoff if Mickelson could make a par.

However, instead of playing conservatively and aiming for a safe par, Mickelson took a bold and risky approach. He attempted an aggressive shot over the trees and water on the left side of the fairway to reach the green in two shots. It was a high-risk, high-reward decision that could have easily ended in disaster.

With nerves of steel, Mickelson executed the shot to perfection, the ball landing safely on the green, setting up a birdie opportunity. He made the birdie putt, securing a one-stroke victory over Ernie Els and winning his first major championship.

Mickelson's daring play on the final hole of the 2004 Masters is now famously known as "The Shot." It showcased his confidence, skill, and willingness to take calculated risks under pressure. The victory was a significant milestone in Mickelson's career, solidifying his place as one of the game's greatest players.

This story serves as a reminder that in golf, as in life, taking risks can lead to great rewards. It's about believing in yourself and seizing opportunities, even when the outcome is uncertain. Mickelson's triumph at the 2004 Masters is a prime example of how taking a bold risk can pay off in the most remarkable and memorable ways.

A study known as The Grant Study, or the Harvard Study of Adult Development, began in 1938 and is still ongoing. It focused on ninety-year-old men, who were asked the question: If you had the chance to live your life all over again, what would you do differently? Their responses can be summarized into three main categories:

1. Reflect more. Get to a park bench, get to a beach, and with no distractions just simply reflect. Ask questions like: What made you sad? What makes you happy? What made you cry? Simply reflect. Remember that to reflect is to restore!

2. Take more risk. For me, that means exercising my faith!

3. The most popular: Invest in things that will outlast you. There are only two things in this world that will last forever: God's Word and His people. The Bible is over three thousand thirty-five years old, created somewhere between 1200 and 165 BC. I believe it's safe to say it will be around forever until Christ comes back for us all who believe.

"Where there is no risk, there is no faith!" What a saying! A good friend, Tim Cooper, shared that with me in a conversation about pursuing opportunities in life and the courage it takes to take the leap. I've taken risks in my career by exploring opportunities beyond my current workplace while pursuing external interests. It involves considering whether the company is a good fit for your skills and the potential financial stability of the company. You have to assess their future prospects and whether their revenue and profit margins can support the overhead costs, including your salary. There are many factors to consider, and it requires you to embrace and become comfortable with the unknown.

Many times, I've found myself staring down the fairway at a body of water protecting the front of the green, going back and forth in my mind on whether I should go for it to the green in two shots instead of three, in order to improve my chances of scoring better on a par 5 hole. It can be intimidating when you start thinking about the risk versus the reward. In some cases, I go for it, while in others, I may not. It depends on a cost-versus-return-on-investment model.

"It was by faith that Abraham obeyed when God called him to leave home and go to another land that God would give him as his inheritance. He went without knowing where he was going. And even when he reached the land God promised him, he lived there by faith, for he was like a foreigner, living in tents," Hebrews 11:8-9.

Look at Sarah's example of risk-based action when she took on the responsibility of having a child at the age of ninety. What would any medical doctor say about that during a doctor's appointment regarding risk? Can you imagine that conversation? God promised Abraham that she would be a mother of nations and that she would conceive and bear a son, Isaac. It was an act of faith. Let's not fear taking risks when God calls us to do so. I'm not saying always go for the green in two swings on a par 5, nor am I saying consider having a child at ninety. However, I do encourage you to seek God's wisdom in all your decisions.

How about considering and evaluating potential benefits and consequences? Consider worst case scenario and whether you can handle it. This is a calculated and assessed risk.

Set clear goals and define what you want to achieve with the risk, ensuring that it aligns with your values and long-term objectives. When I'm considering hitting golf shots to reach the green in two strokes versus three on a par 5, I do consider the worst-case scenario for my score if the ball ends up in a hazard or gets lost. At times, I also think about my current score for the round and the potential score at the end of the round, depending on whether things go well or not. These are factors to consider when taking risks.

Knowledge is a powerful tool. Learn as much as you can about the risk you're taking, which can help you make informed decisions. It can literally take the risk right out of it.

Seek advice. We discussed this on Hole 3: talk to mentors or people with experience in the area where you're taking a risk. Your caddie or personal board of directors can provide valuable insights and guidance.

During my six-month professional development assignment in Shanghai, China, I initiated a one-on-one exit meeting with the general manager of Shanghai General Motors. I asked him, "If you were to give me one piece of advice, what would it be?" His response, "Go with your gut! Always go with your gut!" Trust your intuition. While data and advice are important, trust your gut feeling. Sometimes, your instincts can guide you in the right direction. This was good advice.

Develop a well-thought-out plan that includes contingency measures. Having a plan can reduce some of the anxiety associated with taking risks.

Stay flexible. Be open to adjusting your course if things don't go as planned. Flexibility can help you adapt to unexpected situations. As an avid golfer, and an average golfer, you have to stay flexible on the golf course. More often than not, you will be in a position that's not always the best position. Great golfers adjust very well and stay positive and open-minded. That's the beauty of golf!

Manage fear. It's natural to feel fear when taking risks. Acknowledge your fear, but don't let it paralyze you. Use it as a source of energy and motivation.

All these things will aid you in taking risks, where you'll be able to reflect on your life and see how it served you in so many ways. Swinging back to the theme, "where there is no risk, there is no faith." In certain moments, one must rely on faith. Go after those dreams God has placed in your heart.

In which aspects of your life can you comfortably introduce more risk-taking? _____

_____

_____

_____

_____

_____

_____

_____

_____

What's your current, most significant challenge that demands you to embrace risks and have faith? _____

_____

_____

_____

_____

_____

_____

_____

_____

_____

What actions can you pursue to strengthen your faith? ___

_____

_____

_____

_____

_____

_____

_____

_____

_____

_____

COMMIT

Left It Short

"For all have sinned and fall short of the glory of God, and all are justified freely by his grace through the redemption that came by Christ Jesus."
—Romans 3:23-24

Sometimes, when we're on the green, we become infatuated with the putting line and forget about the speed of the putt. This might happen because of a lack of confidence in our putting stroke, nervousness, or fear. Alternatively, it could be that our putting technique simply isn't up to par. As a result, the putt falls short of reaching the hole. Statistics indicate that every short putt failing to reach the hole never goes in.

In golf, the reality of the game truly sets in on the putting surface on a green when you're closing out a hole, a round, or a tournament for professional golfers. Putting emphasizes that every swing matters in golf, and often, your overall golf score can be greatly influenced on the putting green. As a result, golfers frequently express their emotions passionately in various ways on the putting surface after sinking the putt to complete play on a particular golf hole. Emotions can be expressed through a fist pump for a good score, tossing their golf cap in celebration, or hurling a golf ball into the water in frustration after taking a triple bogey. At times, it is evident a golfer is experiencing joy or anger when completing play on a golf hole.

In the amateur world of golf, I would venture to say that many golfers struggle with the ability to move on from a golf hole where they have scored poorly. They often carry their frustration from that hole to the next one. As humans, we tend to hold onto our frustration or anger for longer than we should, which affects our current and future emotional state. It can also be a challenge for many people to be too hard on themselves and spend too long critiquing and spending time thinking about their past actions seeking improvement or better ways to handle challenges. Reflecting on the past happens for many reasons in multiple areas of our life. Although it is healthy to understand and learn from our shortcomings, it is crucial to do it in a healthy and timely manner. We're human and it is very common to fail in school, at work, in our marriage, or in other areas of our life. For example, when we start a new relationship with someone while carrying experiences and emotions from the previous one, we often use the term "carrying our baggage." Essentially, we're burdened, and this baggage weighs us down, stifling the potential of the new relationship with the new person. Bringing our authentic selves into any relationship becomes difficult when we're carrying the burdens and old memories of pain and suffering of past relationships that did not go so well.

When we leave a putt short on the putting surface, it's in our best interest as golfers to immediately forget about it and move on to the next. Give ourselves some grace and keep it moving. We don't want to carry that negative thought of failure into the next hole when standing on the tee box.

We fail often! We fall short in our decision-making at times. The good news is that God covers us with His grace and mercy. He often protects us from consequences of our poor choices or behavior. We're not perfect. It's inevitable a golfer will leave a putt short. We will come short of reaching some of our goals. We are all sinners. However, He has already paid the price for our sins, and we are no longer slaves to sin. We don't have to beat ourselves up over of the mistakes we've made or the sins we've committed. We can let go of that burden and give it to God. As a result, we can live more freely and truly live.

2 Chronicles 7:14 states that those who are called by His name to humble themselves, turn from their wicked ways, pray sincerely, seeking His face so that their sins can be forgiven, and they can be healed. 1 John 1:9 reads, "*If we confess our sins, he is faithful and just and will forgive us our sins*

and purify us from all unrighteousness." Discuss it with some of your personal board of director members. Phone a friend. Share with that person what you are struggling with and be open to advice, or simply a comforting word.

Let's be clear. I'm not saying that leaving a putt short is a sin. What I am saying is that as hard as we try to do what's right and pleasing to God, it is impossible not to sin, make mistakes, or simply fail at times because we're human. My encouragement to you is that we shouldn't carry all of those burdens around with us. That's heavy!

"Come to me, all of you who are weary and burdened, and I will give you rest. Take my yoke upon you and learn from me, for I am gentle and humble in heart, and you will find rest for your souls. For my yoke is easy and my burden is light," (Matthew 11:28-30). It would be good to have God as our caddie in this sense, where He is willing and would love to carry our burdens while we hit our best shots around the course. Translation: Partner with God in every aspect of your life. He's always there and looking ahead of you guiding you on the course of life.

When we find ourselves missing a putt, leaving it short, or committing a sin, falling short of the glory of God, we should spend as little time as possible dwelling on it—certainly much less time than it takes to walk from the green on the hole where you missed the putt to the tee box on the next hole.

God loves us and desires what is best for us and His purpose for our lives. We thrive when we are our authentic selves, carrying fewer of our past mistakes, bad experiences, and tough moments from our past. We move quicker and with more intention. Stay committed to God. Repent and turn to God so that your sins can be wiped out, allowing times of refreshing to come from the Lord (Acts 3:19). Give him your burdens; He'll do the heavy lifting for you. It's a new hole! It's a new round! It's a new day!

In a serene, distraction-free environment, such as your favorite spot at home, where interruptions are far from reach, I invite you to engage in the following:

- Assume a posture of humility and comfort, perhaps on your knees. This position will help you achieve a sense of solitude for a few minutes, maybe even with the palms of your hands in an open position, facing upward. After clearing your mind of distractions, envision yourself in the presence of God.

- Now that you have connected with God, share with Him your challenges and concerns that may be weighing heavily on your heart.

- Experience the weight of those burdens being gently lifted from your body and mind, and imagine a compassionate, reassuring smile from God. Know that these concerns are now in God's hands, and He will carry them for you.

- Have faith and trust in the wisdom of a greater plan for your life and believe in the unfolding of the process.

COMMIT

Everything in the Bag

"Whatever you do, work at it with all your heart, as working for the Lord, not for human masters, since you know that you will receive an inheritance from the Lord as a reward. It is the Lord Christ you are serving."
—Colossians 3:23-24

I recall playing a hole several years ago. It was a 585-yard par 5. I crushed my drive off the tee, positioning my ball 285 yards to the green from the center of the fairway. I had an opportunity to go for it in two shots instead of settling for a standard, somewhat boring three.

For the non-golfer, a par 5 golf hole is designed for the average golfer to take three golf shots for their ball to arrive on the green. At that point, the golfer has an opportunity to putt twice to achieve what the course has designed for that hole to be considered successful. If it takes fewer shots to reach the hole, it increases the chances to score better than what the course designer intended, which is a great thing!

In this case, there were a couple of bunkers on both sides of the green, but no trouble at all between me and the green. My friend asked me, "What club will you use to try to get it to the hole?" I shouted out, "Everything in the bag!" We both burst into laughter because he and I knew I had to hit my longest fairway club, other than the driver, and hit the ball dead center of the club face with significant club head speed.

I pulled it off but ended up with a two-putt for birdie, versus a one-putt eagle. Go figure. The reward to any golfer when going for a green in two on a par 5 hole is to capitalize an opportunity to one putt for an eagle score. This is two shots less than the hole intends for it to take. It's an amazing score on any course and on any hole.

Sometimes, a golf shot demands that you give it your all, leaving nothing in the tank. You must risk it all, fully committing and dedicating yourself to the shot. What, in your life, is worth putting it all on the line for? Your family members? Your dreams?

In his book, *The 7 Habits of Highly Effective People*, Stephen Covey posed the question, of which I'm paraphrasing: "What would be worth the risk of death on the other end of a tightrope walk suspended between two skyscrapers in New York City? What would be awaiting you once you make it to the other side?"

For me, it's about attaining and claiming what's most important to me, whether it's my family, my purpose, or elements that contribute to my brand and legacy. A good self-check involves reviewing your calendar over the past few months to see if the activities you've been involved in align with and contribute to those things for which you're willing to take risks and make sacrifices. While you may never physically walk a tightrope at those dizzying heights to achieve or possess them, mentally going through this exercise can provide valuable insights. It can reveal something within you, and at times, it can feel like a faith walk in our lives and should be embraced as such.

There are moments when we're compelled to exercise our faith in our actions, whether at work, at home, in the community, or elsewhere. However, there are also opportunities when we choose to take risks and wholeheartedly depend on God's power to assist us in our endeavors or help us overcome our challenges. When are you giving it your all? I'd imagine it is something you love. It may be something you're extremely good at. It could be something purposeful or something God has called you to do. Perhaps it's a loved one that needs you to take on a task that benefits them. There are many things I'd imagine and for different reasons.

As I mentioned earlier, I hold a deep love for God, my family, people, and golf. These aspects of my life are profoundly important to me. During most interactions with family and friends, I'm constantly on the lookout for opportunities to encourage and guide people toward God. It's a personal mission, one that requires confidence and a delicate touch to avoid offending anyone or pushing them away. My love for my family and the desire for everlasting relationships with them make it a worthy risk and a sacrifice.

Approaching people about their faith carries inherent risks, including the possibility that they may limit their interactions with me as a result. However, I've accepted that risk, and it undeniably requires faith. I want people to realize their full potential in anything to which they aspire or for which they possess a talent. I'm willing to make sacrifices, whether in terms of time or money, to assist in any way I can. If it demands taking risks, such as how people perceive me or even the potential risk of my job, it's worth everything in my bag to do what I love and help others along the way.

God is greater than the risk; He'll help you with whatever you're attempting if you seek him first. He's greater than any problem you'll ever face, and He'll support you along the way. 2 Timothy 1:7 says, *"For God gave us a spirit not of fear but of power and love and self-control."* There was no fear when I hit that 285-yard, 3-wood shot to reach the green. There couldn't have been, as the results would've been much different, if not punitive. That's the mindset we must adopt in our personal and professional lives—giving it our all and changing our thinking as if it's already a reality. We should imagine that ball on the green before striking it, envision that promotion before it's offered, and picture whatever it is as if it already exists. Ephesians 3:20 is one of my favorite verses, and I pray it daily to etch it into my mind: *"Now to him who is able to do far more abundantly than all that we can ask or think, according to the power at work within us, to him be the glory in the church and in Christ Jesus throughout all generations, forever and ever."* Amen. If that's not leveraging everything in the bag, I don't know what is. You can achieve anything in your life by simply giving it to Him if it's His will, not yours.

What endeavor right now necessitates your complete dedication and unshakeable faith? _____

_____

_____

_____

_____

_____

_____

_____

_____

_____

Identify the risks and assess both the potential rewards and consequences. Provide a list of these items below. _____

_____

_____

_____

_____

_____

_____

_____

_____

_____

List below steps needed to reach completion of your endeavor.

_____

_____

_____

_____

_____

_____

_____

_____

_____

_____

FOLLOW THROUGH

Stay in the Slot

"Have I not commanded you? Be strong and courageous. Do not be afraid; do not be discouraged, for the Lord your God will be with you wherever you go."
—Joshua 1:9

"Stay in the slot" has to be one of the most epic swing mechanic slogans in the game of golf, and one of the most critical aspects of the swing pattern to have a chance at hitting a pure shot. If you come out of it during the downswing of a golf shot, it can wreak havoc on hitting the ball squarely.

Similarly, staying in God's Word is a great and an absolute amazing place to be. Staying in God's Word doesn't guarantee a smooth, care-free life with no challenges, pain, or suffering. However, staying connected to God through His Word, coupled with His grace and mercy, will see you through difficult times. It will strengthen your relationship with Him over time and bring about calmness and peace.

Just like staying in the slot mitigates errant golf shots, staying in God's Word mitigates sin. It deepens our understanding of our faith and helps us grow spiritually. It provides guidance, wisdom, and insight into living a righteous and fulfilling life. God's Word is a moral and ethical compass. Just like our GPS is in golf, the Bible offers the moral and ethical framework that can help us make better choices in our personal and social environments with principles and teachings on how to live justly and compassionately. It gives us hope and comforts us in affliction and inspires us. I find solace and encouragement in the stories, verses, and messages in difficult times. No matter the circumstances, you can find peace in God's Word. On the other hand, if you don't stay in God's Word, you will become lost.

Not being connected to God or reading His Word opens up the opportunity and risk of sinning more. You can experience spiritual stagnation. Without regular engagement you may miss out on opportunities for personal growth, deeper understanding of your faith, and a closer relationship with benefits thereof. You can potentially make questionable immoral choices. Lastly, you miss comfort and inspiration. In times of adversity or uncertainty, you lack a source of solace and it can be difficult as a result. The farther you are from God, the more painful those difficult times are. The closer you are to God, the less painful it is. The struggle increases in battling sin, finding comfort and strength in God, and serving

Jesus. 1 Peter 2:2 tells us to stay in God's Word as "newborn babies thirst for milk." By doing so, we grow as Christians. The word of God is our anchor, tethering our minds to the truth and serving as a source of faith.

God's Word provides key verses to combat various adverse situations when they arise. You'll have these verses for yourself, and others if needed, and you'll be able to recall them quickly, just as Jesus did when the devil tempted him on three occasions, as I learned in Matthew 4:1-11:

"Then Jesus was led up by the Spirit into the wilderness to be tempted by the devil. ² And when He had fasted forty days and forty nights, afterward He was hungry. ³ Now when the tempter came to Him, he said, "If You are the Son of God, command that these stones become bread."

⁴ But He answered and said, "It is written, 'Man shall not live by bread alone, but by every word that proceeds from the mouth of God.' "

⁵ Then the devil took Him up into the holy city, set Him on the pinnacle of the temple, ⁶ and said to Him, "If You are the Son of God, throw Yourself down. For it is written:

'He shall give His angels charge over you,'

and,

'In their hands they shall bear you up, Lest you dash your foot against a stone.'"

⁷ Jesus said to him, "It is written again, 'You shall not [a]tempt the Lord your God.'"

⁸ Again, the devil took Him up on an exceedingly high mountain, and showed Him all the kingdoms of the world and their glory. ⁹ And he said to Him, "All these things I will give You if You will fall down and worship me."

¹⁰ Then Jesus said to him, "Away with you, Satan! For it is written, 'You shall worship the LORD your God, and Him only you shall serve.'"

¹¹ Then the devil left Him, and behold, angels came and ministered to Him.

The devil tried once more, but Jesus, armed with scripture in his heart and mind, successfully resisted the devil's temptation. We learn so much from these examples, knowing that we too need to read God's Word repeatedly to have it in our hearts and minds to fight the temptations that will come throughout our lives. These temptations could potentially separate us from our purpose, our missions, and our goals.

Just as in golf, where we need a full bag of clubs for all the shots we might face on the course, we must have the full armor of God on daily to fend off and overcome the devil's schemes. While you continue working hard and waiting for results or breakthroughs, keep asking God until they come. Keep knocking on the door, as Jesus advised his disciples in Luke 11:9-13.

Remember, God's timing is perfect timing. As you follow through on all the things you set out to do in life, finish strong with hope, faith, and belief in yourself and in God. As stated in Philippians 1:6, be confident of this very thing, *"He who has begun a good work in you will complete it until the day of Jesus Christ."* God isn't done with you yet! It now makes sense to me when I've heard of a person's tombstone reading, "Construction complete."

Joshua received God's command four times in Chapter 1 of the book of Joshua in the Bible. This happened when he took over from Moses after Moses's death and became the leader of the Israelites, guiding them to the promised land. God instructed him to be strong and courageous; not to fear or be discouraged. Joshua was told to meditate on God's Word day and night and to follow His instructions, with the promise that he would find success wherever he went.

To translate this for us, it means we should diligently spend time with God by reading His Word and following His teachings. We should remain in God's Word, be prayerful, and stay alert. By continuing to meditate on His Word and seeking His guidance, we should strive to do our best and obey His instructions. John 15:7-8 reinforces this message, stating that if we abide in God and His Word remains in us, we can ask for anything, and it will be done for us. This glorifies God, and we bear much fruit, proving ourselves to be His disciples. We should trust God, rest in His promises; keep asking, praying, and taking action.

God's Word is described as refreshing to our souls. An analogy that illustrates this well is imagining being on a raft at the beach, just offshore from your family, who are on the sand about 100 yards away. As you start to drift in thought, you lose focus on staying directly across from your family. Neglecting to paddle and maintain your position in the water causes you to drift a mile away while your family remains staked out on the sand. This is similar to not reading God's Word and spending daily time with Him. You may drift away from your connection and relationship with God, even though He hasn't moved; you have. However, as we spend more time in God's Word, our focus returns to Him, and our souls are nourished. Our relationship with God is renewed, as mentioned in Psalms 19:7, *"The law of the Lord is perfect, reviving the soul; the testimony of the Lord is sure, making wise the simple."*

I would venture to say that just as staying in the slot provides a pure shot, staying in God's Word grants us wisdom! God has provided answers to all of life's important questions in His Word. 2 Peter 1:3 states, *"His divine power has given us everything we need for a godly life through our knowledge of him who called us by his own glory and goodness."* He has given us His precious and great promises, so that we may become participants in the divine nature.

Hitting a pure shot in golf, as a result of staying in the slot, brings immense joy. It's an amazing feeling, knowing you've aligned key aspects of your swing to hit a great shot. Conversely, when a shot goes awry, it's a clear indication that something went wrong with one or more of those swing mechanics. It's an incredible feeling, knowing that you've keyed your swing to achieve greatness. It's fascinating to observe golfers who, after hitting a poor shot, meticulously analyze their swings in slow motion, attempting to pinpoint the cause.

As an avid golfer, I can relate, and I often find parallels between golf and life's challenges. When facing obstacles in life, my initial response is to reflect on my relationship with God. I revisit the fundamental principles of my faith and ask myself important questions. Am I spending time with Him daily? Am I seeking Him first in all things? Is He the center of my life? Am I immersing myself in His Word?

To clarify, I'm not suggesting that your current situation is a direct result of poor choices. Life is unpredictable, and unforeseen events occur. However, how you navigate through these situations significantly impacts your experience of God's peace amid adversity. Focus on the eternal rather than the short term. Let go of what you can't control. Remember the wisdom from Philippians 4:6: *"Be anxious for nothing, but in everything by prayer and supplication, with thanksgiving, let your requests be made known to God."*

Staying grounded in God's Word promises a joy far greater than achieving the perfect golf swing. Embrace His Word!

How connected do you feel to God at the moment? _____

_____

_____

_____

_____

When do you feel closest to God? _____

_____

_____

_____

_____

Do you actively engage with God's Word daily? _____

_____

_____

_____

_____

If not, what steps are you willing to take now to ensure a lasting commitment to reading His Word in your life? ____

_____

_____

_____

_____

FOLLOW THROUGH

Finish High and Let It Fly

"They that wait upon the Lord shall renew their strength, they shall mount up with wings of eagles, they shall run and not be weary, they shall walk, and not faint."
—Isaiah 40:31

How many things have you initiated but left unfinished? As you ponder on that question, consider the various things required to complete any task or project. These may encompass factors such as time, finances, motivation, and various intangible or tangible resources.

When I reflect on Isaiah 40:31, the concept of strength stands out prominently. It portrays a person standing tall in readiness and preparedness to undertake a potentially time-consuming and physically or mentally demanding endeavor. Isaiah gives you perhaps a sense of urgency while also encouraging patience and trust in God's unwavering promises and faithfulness.

The message is clear: Keep going. Persevere. Do not falter, and bring a good dose of strength along with you.

Similarly, there's nothing like teeing off and watching the ball soar through the air down the center of the fairway when you generate power, refrain from holding back, and persist in your swing. At that moment, you can immediately feel the outcomes of strength, diligent practice, unwavering focus, and relaxation all coming together after a successful strike.

A dedicated golfer will encounter numerous golf clichés throughout their years playing the sport. As a golfer sets up their ball on a golf tee on a tee box, you might often hear advice from a fellow golfer: "Tee it high and let it fly!" It is a phrase of encouragement to swing with strength. You witness the results of your powerful swing and follow-through, and you patiently anticipate where it will ultimately land—likely in the fairway, just as you intended. Some golfers may react to that well-struck tee shot by exclaiming, "You really sent that one!" Additionally, someone else might say, "You placed that ball right there in the mayor's office!"

If your swing, particularly during the upward or follow-through phase, embodies the qualities of power, strength, and grace, the ball will take off and generally find a favorable position.

When comparing these swing principles to the goals, projects, or assignments you may encounter in your personal or professional life, it becomes evident that strength is a crucial factor when it comes to completing tasks and meeting your expectations. Reflecting on over eighty percent of my golf rounds where my score fell short of my desired outcome, I've come to realize that, more often than not, something changed unfavorably between holes 15 and 18 for various reasons. I could not finish the round strong because of not playing those final three holes well, resulting in a less favorable golf score.

These reasons are often linked to factors such as a lack of physical strength, diminished stamina, and lapses in focus, among others. An example of a lapse in focus could be where you look at your scorecard mid-way or near the end of your golf round and realize you're having exceptional round! You then proceed to hit an errant golf shot to ruin the score on that hole, and ultimately eliminate the chances of it being the round of your life.

In this chapter, I aim to emphasize discovering and securing the strength required to finish strong—a metaphorical representation of the final holes in a golf game. Strength to follow through empowers you to overcome obstacles such as lapses in focus, diminished stamina, and other challenges, ensuring successful navigation towards finishing. As Isaiah 40:31 tells us, *"For those who wait upon the Lord, they shall renew their strength. They will run and not be weary, walk and not faint."* This is an encouraging message for people of faith, assuring us that our strength will be restored when we depend on God.

When you put your trust in Him, not only will your physical health be restored, but your overall well-being, your career, and your relationships as well. You can find this strength in His Word through reading, prayer, and meditation, no matter what challenges life has thrown your way, whether it's health issues, job difficulties, relationship strains, or simply a few challenging holes left to finish 18 holes of some magnificent golf.

God will see you through it, providing resources if necessary and creating alternative paths when faced with dead ends. 1 Chronicles 16:11 tells us to *"Seek the Lord and His strength; seek His presence continually."* He will neither leave us nor forsake us. We can do all things through Him who strengthens us, says Philippians 4:13. Tap into this source, rejuvenate your spirit, and restore and replenish your strength!

There are various ways to achieve this; your choice should align with your current life situation. A good starting point might involve connecting with your board of directors and seeking the advice needed to help you follow through and complete what you've started. In my marriage, when my wife and I face rough patches, we connect, reflect, and build on the fundamental values that have sustained us over the years. We seek God and apply the principles He taught us— kindness, patience, humility, and forgiveness, as exemplified in Ephesians 4:32. It's amazing how reconnecting with a source that surpasses any other can revive your marriage or any relationship you hold dear.

Practice regularly, take lessons, play with others, and focus on your mental game. Work on developing mental toughness and focus, which can help you stay calm and composed during high-pressure situations during a golf round, providing strength in your golf game. The same principles apply to strengthening your faith. Read regularly, pray consistently, and connect with others, perhaps through a Bible study group.

When faced with challenges in my life, I sometimes turn to fasting. Fasting is a powerful spiritual discipline, and through fasting and prayer, the Holy Spirit can transform your situation or life. The practice of fasting has deep roots in the Bible. Even Jesus himself spent time fasting and praying during his life on Earth, and He expects believers to fast as well (Matthew 6:16). This can be done in various ways and at different levels of intensity, depending on how the Holy Spirit moves you, either for personal growth or specific requests.

Fasting helps us realize that all we need is God, and it reminds us to seek Him first in everything we do, ensuring that we depend on Him for strength to follow through on all our endeavors.

Another effective way to strengthen your faith is by connecting with your community and actively participating in community gatherings. Engaging in acts of kindness is another powerful method. I met a gentleman who owns a restaurant in our community, and he shared a remarkable story with my wife and me. In February 2021, in the largest historical deep freeze in Austin, Texas, he witnessed the dire circumstances of the homeless population. They were without heat, food, or water, and tragically, he saw twenty people lose their lives.

In response, he decided to do what he believed was right. He gave each of the homeless individuals $20 to help them and also gave one of them a jacket he had received twenty years earlier from his brother, which held sentimental value. During extreme weather conditions like freezing temperatures, a jacket can mean a lot more than $20 to someone without shelter. These experiences significantly strengthened his faith, and just hearing about it has had a positive impact on me. It has increased my sensitivity to helping those in need, aligning with what God calls us to do as Christians living out our faith.

Matthew further reinforces our Christian duties when Jesus is speaking in Matthew 25:34-40:

'Then the King will say to those on his right, "Come, you who are blessed by my Father; take your inheritance, the kingdom prepared for you since the creation of the world. 35 For I was hungry and you gave me something to eat, I was thirsty and you gave me something to drink, I was a stranger and you invited me in, 36 I needed clothes and you clothed me, I was ill and you looked after me, I was in prison and you came to visit me."

37 'Then the righteous will answer him, "Lord, when did we see you hungry and feed you, or thirsty and give you something to drink? 38 When did we see you a stranger and invite you in, or needing clothes and clothe you? [39] *When did we see you ill or in prison and go to visit you?"*

[40] *"The King will reply, "Truly I tell you, whatever you did for one of the least of these brothers and sisters of mine, you did for me."*

This is how you strengthen your walk of faith!

Study and reflect on your beliefs. Prayer and meditation will help you achieve this! Finding a quiet place and spending some of the most valuable time assessing your heart, your current position, and where you'd like to be.

Seek opportunities to share your faith and engage in acts of kindness. Additionally, seek guidance from trusted sources and work on developing a growth mindset rather than fearing failure.

Set achievable goals, celebrate progress, and learn from setbacks. Practice self-care, both mentally and physically, by ensuring you get enough sleep, eat well, exercise regularly, and prioritize self-care activities.

Cultivate positive self-talk by replacing negative thoughts with positive affirmations, and focus on your strengths and accomplishments. All of these practices will provide you with the tools you need to move forward and accomplish both small and large goals.

Finishing on a high note can either enhance a good round or salvage it. Find strength and finish strong!

From where do you presently draw the strength required to complete what you have initiated? _____

_____

_____

_____

_____

_____

_____

_____

Consider engaging in activities in your community or afar as mentioned in this chapter that can bolster your faith. Please list those and put them into practice. _____

_____

_____

_____

_____

_____

_____

_____

_____

Hole
16

FOLLOW THROUGH

Focus

"He said, 'Come.' So Peter got out of the boat and walked on water and came to Jesus. But when he saw the wind, he was afraid, and beginning to sink he cried out, 'Lord, save me...' 'O you of little faith, why did you doubt?'"
—Matthew 14: 29-31

Focus! Throughout my life, I've had the privilege of meeting hundreds, if not thousands, of people. Among them, a few individuals, some very close to me, stand out for their laser-like focus. One such person is Mickey Washington, a former NFL football player, with an eight-year career, who has since become an attorney running his own firm. Mickey's level of focus is truly remarkable and unmatched, and it has earned him numerous accolades both on and off the gridiron. Late in his football career, he received the "Unsung Hero" award from the Jacksonville Jaguars, and he has been recognized as the Super Lawyer of the Year in Houston, Texas, on at least two occasions in 2018 and 2023. I've had the opportunity to speak with Mickey and ask him to describe what focus meant to him. His response made perfect sense and yielded some amazing returns on his investment of focus in his career.

Mickey shared from an early age, he felt God guiding him to aim higher, motivating him to excel both as a defensive back and occasionally as an offensive running back. Just like in the follow through of a golf swing, reaching higher will create a swing plane that will influence a higher ball flight once the ball is struck.

He stated that he was inspired to utilize every gift God had given him. His work ethic, hunger, and desire to elevate on all aspects of his life helped him grow closer to God. It strengthened his relationship with God, while he learned more about himself at a deeper level.

Mickey explained his work ethic and NFL aspirations, comparing his desire for success to the urgency as if his head was being held underwater, needing to come up for a breath. He learned that from R.M. Drake, a contemporary American author, poet, and social media influencer. As a result of being vertically challenged at the height of five-foot-nine, coupled with the fact that he was not the fastest, strongest, nor biggest defensive back, it drove intense workout habits that resulted in eight years in the National Football League.

Mickey would study the teams' top-rated cornerbacks' style of play, their routines, how they studied the game, and their work ethics. He literally took pages out of their book.

What also sharpened Mickey's focus was his standard work of committing to finding a bible study group on each NFL team he played for. He knew there was at least one on each team that existed. Mickey said it was pertinent in his life to keep that laser focus and be tethered to God's direction for his life.

He would also conduct spiritual fasts during both the season and off-season. We discussed this practice on an earlier hole. He learned this from Jesus. Spiritual fasting is a practice observed in various religious and spiritual traditions where individuals voluntarily abstain from certain foods, activities, or behaviors for a specific period of time as a way of deepening their connection with a higher power, achieve spiritual growth, and gain a clearer perspective on life. In Mickey's case, he connected with God and requested clarity on His purpose for his life. He would accompany that fast with prayer, meditation, self-reflection, and contemplation. As a result, Mickey gained a state of mindfulness, humility, and self-discipline which showed up on the football field and off! I actually participated in my very first fast with Mickey in my early twenties during college, seeking God's wisdom. I do it periodically when I seemed to have lost focus whether in my career, my relationship with my wife, or when I feel far away from God. It helps me tremendously to regain my focus.

Lastly, rounding out the factors that kept Mickey focused, especially during his NFL career and continuing into his legal profession, was the abundant love and support he received when visiting his hometown and nearby cities. Former local barbers, coaches, and fans who witnessed his play consistently encouraged him without limits. This is how Mickey best described focus. It can be defined or described many ways and look and sound differently to many people.

Golf requires an unwavering focus on every single shot, whether it's a putt, an iron shot, or a fairway wood, whether you're on the tee box or navigating the rough off the fairway. Any golf pro will affirm that the game of golf leans heavily on mental prowess rather than sheer physical skill. Focus, in this context, means dedicating your full attention and concentration. It demands your heart and must reside at the core of your mind. The challenge then is to attain full engagement and persistently focus on your dreams and goals. How do you stay unwaveringly committed to the actions that lead to success, whether in the realm of golf or in your personal and professional life?

Let's begin by acknowledging the reality of what we struggle with when it comes to maintaining focus. Paul articulates it best in Ephesians 6:12, *"For our struggle is not against the flesh and blood, but against the rulers, against the authorities, against the powers of this dark world and against the spiritual forces of evil in the heavenly realms."* This is the stark reality we face day in and day out. This scripture provides the right perspective and helps us channel our focus correctly.

Despite this challenging reality, it's also very encouraging to read what follows: *"Finally, brothers and sisters, whatever is true, whatever is noble, whatever is right, whatever is pure, whatever is lovely, whatever is admirable—if anything is excellent or praiseworthy - think about such things,"* (Philippians 4:8). There could be an entire class dedicated to understanding how to remain vigilant in doing the very things that God has requested of us through Paul's writing. We must be intentional, even in our thoughts.

At different times, in various positions, or when dealing with different tasks, different types of focus are required. Similar to Mickey Washington, golfers must maintain a strong focus, staying in the present moment on every shot and throughout the entire round. They should avoid dwelling on past shots or thinking about the next one. It's essential not to let unrelated experiences intrude on the golf round unless they bring positivity and harmony to the game.

I've listened to gospel music during many of my rounds, which brings a sense of peace and calmness to my mind, setting the tempo of my game where it needs to be. You'd think I'd do it every time! Generally, skilled golfers don't dwell on their swing mechanics or the score they hope to achieve. They certainly avoid thoughts that could frustrate them. All of these aspects contribute to their ability to maintain the necessary focus to play well.

In every endeavor, focus is required to some extent. We must not only adjust our level of focus, depending on the task but also be capable of fending off distractions and deterrents. The devil constantly seeks ways to derail us. As I mentioned earlier, morning is the best opportunity for me to spend time with God and take care of my health. I've created a conducive environment that minimizes interruptions and ensures I don't take away from my family.

What are the areas in your life that demand focus? Is it your purpose, finances, relationships, or faith? Is it your work?

Peter excelled as long as he kept his gaze fixed on Jesus; he achieved the impossible by walking on water, a miracle matched only by Jesus Himself in His human form. Peter's unwavering focus allowed him to achieve this remarkable feat. Hebrews 12:2 emphasizes the need to *"Fix our eyes on Jesus, the pioneer and perfecter of faith."* This requires continuous renewal of our minds and thoughts, staying alert and sober, and placing our hope in Jesus' grace (1 Peter 1:13). Proverbs 4:25 says, *"Let your eyes look straight ahead; fix your gaze directly before you."* These passages offer valuable insights into maintaining daily focus throughout our lives on Earth. Keep the faith! Don't lose sight of your aspirations and goals, which you pursue using the gifts God has given you. In the face of discouragement or fear, resist the devil's influence and remain steadfastly locked into your focus. A true and unwavering focus on your objectives brings immense joy and fulfillment.

Making the necessary adjustments to attain clarity in focus is imperative. Setting boundaries and restrictions to ward off distractions, disbelief, fear, doubt, and negativity, which are not aligned with God, is equally vital as these factors can obscure your vision and diminish your focus. Creating an environment conducive to maintaining focus on your desired task is essential. Peter provides an excellent illustration of an unwavering focus on God as well as a stark example of faltering faith during the same event when he allowed doubt to infiltrate his mind while walking on water toward Jesus. There is much to learn from both aspects of his experience.

Identifying doubts or distractions that may be creeping into your mind, potentially delaying or disrupting your focus, is essential. Respond promptly and resolutely to counter these fears, doubts, or distractions, and regain your center. It starts in your mind. Self-assessments can help you stay alert to recognize these challenges and act against them. These challenges may include addictions, temptations, sinful desires, and more. 1 Peter 5:8 serves as a reminder to *"Be alert and of sober mind,"* as the devil prowls like a roaring lion, seeking to devour anyone.

Every day, it is crucial to put on our spiritual armor to align our focus with God's will and sustain it over time. Being sober-minded, keeping our heads clear, focused, and intentional in our daily actions places us in an advantageous position, as we discussed earlier. Poor decisions carry consequences that may impair and obscure your vision and focus on God, causing you to miss your target.

Throughout my life, and as I stated earlier, I have often set aside dedicated time and made sacrifices to enhance my focus on God through fasting. Fasting involves committing to a specific duration, whether days or weeks, during which you either eliminate certain habits from your life or incorporate specific actions to intensify your prayer, meditation, and focus on God. For instance, you might abstain from eating burgers for a week or a month or limit your beverage choices to water for an extended period, avoiding sugary or carbonated drinks. During these times, you replace temptations or habits with prayer and spending time with God. The intention is to eliminate idols, break strongholds, cultivate better habits, and minimize detrimental behaviors in particular areas of your life, ultimately becoming a better servant to God, improving your health, and benefiting others. It's also a time to express your needs and desires, humbly and sincerely, to God, especially when you are facing challenges in relationships, career, finances, or other aspects of life. Typically, my focus on God is a correlation on how well I prioritize what truly matters most not only to me but to my loved ones. Get focused!

- Set a schedule for yourself to pray, meditate, and visualize your goals. It can be daily, weekly, or monthly, or beyond.

- Create a vision board: a visual representation of your long-term goals to keep them top of mind.

- Consider fasting. Start with gradual steps and consult your primary physician, especially if it's related to your diet. While fasting, seek guidance and clarity by praying to God for direction in your requests to Him.

FOLLOW THROUGH

Hold Your Line!

"If we die with Him, we will also live with Him. If we endure hardship, we will also reign with Him. If we deny Him, He also will deny us. If we are unfaithful, He remains faithful for He cannot deny Himself!"
—2 Timothy 2:11-13

If you can visualize this scenario with me: the average golfer has just struck the ball off the tee, and their ball is flying perilously close to the right or left side of the fairway, hugging the tree line or out-of-bounds stakes. In a humorous moment, the golfer yells, "Hold your line!" Hilarious! Their body language, particularly their head is attempting to influence the ball's flight path, as if demanding that the ball maintain its relationship with that tree line or out-of-bounds area and not veer any farther away from its position relative to a place more desired. Hence, the phrase, "Hold your line!" While not a common phrase in golf, it's a choice of words that has stuck with me over the years. When I experience this act, it's about hope. Maintaining the hope that the ball will stay in play when you're teeing off or hitting any golf shot on the course, ensuring it doesn't go out of bounds or into undesirable areas.

Holding your finish in a golf swing tends to become easier with practice and experience in playing golf. It's a critical and essential aspect of reinforcing a good-to-great swing and often results in a favorable ball flight pattern. It's a must!

In March 2015, my dad battled Amyloidosis, a rare disease that affects organs by causing an accumulation of amyloid proteins. In his case, it was his heart that was impacted. Over the course of three years, his health slowly deteriorated, and he eventually ended up in the hospital during his final days.

During those last couple of weeks in the hospital, I spent precious moments with him, reading the Bible, praying, and reflecting on our lives and our relationship. I have a vivid memory of one particular day when I was shaving and trimming his beard. As I carefully worked with the clippers, the room was filled with an almost reverent silence.

Then he spoke, with his eyes still closed. "I am so proud of you boys." He was referring to his three sons: my older brother, my twin brother, and me.

After a brief pause, with a tear rolling down my cheek, I replied, "We are a reflection of you!"

He didn't say anything more, and I continued trimming his beard. It was a profoundly touching moment for both of us, reminiscent of Proverbs 17:6, which states, *"Grandchildren are the crown of the aged, and the glory of children is their fathers."*

Our conversation continued that day and for the next couple of weeks, until I had to return home to my family in California. A few days before his passing, my mom called my brothers and me, expressing her concerns about Dad's deteriorating condition. He had stopped eating, and his vital signs were steadily declining. She allowed us to speak with the doctor to ask any questions we had.

I asked the doctor, "What are the chances he could get strong enough to come out of the hospital and return home on a scale of 1 to 10?" Ten, of course, being he would leave the hospital.

The doctor responded, "Negative two." The prognosis was grim for various reasons.

Armed with this information, Mom and I decided to talk to Dad about it the following day, intending to share the doctor's bleak assessment. When we finally had him on the phone, finding the right words was an agonizing struggle. We started with simple inquiries about his well-being and how he was feeling. Gradually, we steered the conversation toward the difficult topic, letting him know what the doctor had said.

That's when I told my dad, "Hold your line!"

His immediate response was filled with a mix of determination and nostalgia. "I got the hook in him!"

It was a phrase we had exchanged for years during our fishing trips whenever we had a big catch on the fishing line. It's phrase that instills a positive and optimistic feeling or expectation that something desired will happen or a situation will in fact improve. We had hope that day, and the days following. We had a belief that a positive outcome is possible, even when we both knew there was uncertainty or challenges ahead of him without a doubt. That exchange of words between my Dad and I was a source of mental and physical strength.

There are numerous ways to finish strong in projects, sports, golf, and in your faith. God will never leave you or forsake you (Hebrews 13:5). He will fight for you and meet you where you are, regardless of the circumstances. Your part is to do your best, and God will do His. We all fall short of the glory of God, but His grace is always sufficient, and He will provide. Keep praying, as it will strengthen your faith and give you strength. When you pray, share your heart's desires and be specific.

In my family's experience, we held onto hope for my dad even when the doctors' prognosis seemed bleak. Looking back on March 2015, I have no regrets about keeping hope and faith in God. It gave me joy. I now believe that God orchestrated the entire journey, including the scripture my dad and I read together during his last days. Those verses became the words I recited to him as he took his last breaths. Every time I revisit them, I find peace. These words are from Paul's writing in Romans 8:35-39:

Who shall separate us from the love of Christ? Shall trouble or hardship or persecution or famine or nakedness or danger or sword? [36] *As it is written:*

'For your sake we face death all day long; we are considered as sheep to be slaughtered.' [a]

[37] *No, in all these things we are more than conquerors through him who loved us.* [38] *For I am convinced that neither death nor life, neither angels nor demons,* [b] *neither the present nor the future, nor any powers,* [39] *neither height nor depth, nor anything else in all creation, will be able to separate us from the love of God that is in Christ Jesus our Lord.*

This is how you hold your line, keep your head high, and maintain strength and faith in anything you do, no matter what challenges come your way. Dig deep, persevere, and keep the hope!

Place your hopes and faith in God to receive what you desire.

What are you hoping for? _____

_____

_____

_____

_____

_____

_____

Think about how you can practice gratitude, using positive affirmations, and setting goals to nurture and sustain hope in your daily life and write those below:

_____

_____

_____

_____

_____

_____

_____

_____

_____

_____

_____

_____

_____

_____

_____

_____

_____

_____

_____

_____

_____

FOLLOW THROUGH

Finish It!

"After this, Jesus, knowing that all things were now accomplished, that the Scripture might be fulfilled, said, 'I thirst!'...So when Jesus had received the sour wine, He said, 'It is finished!'"
—John 19: 28-30

In the summer of 2018, I traveled to Sterling Heights, Michigan, to visit my twin brother, Kevin. Quite often when I visit him, we typically arrange for multiple rounds of golf. For this particular trip, Kevin had arranged for former National Football League player and Hall of Famer, Barry Sanders, to join us for a round of golf at one of the private golf courses in Detroit, Michigan. It was my request to spend some time with Barry on the golf course and give him a token of thanks for his nice gesture in donating his autographed football jersey to NEGU (Never Ever Give Up), a non-profit organization dedicated to children battling cancer and other serious illnesses in Orange County, California.

I was super excited prior to taking off for the trip and was sharing this with one of my personal board of directors, Tony Jonas. Tony could hear the excitement in my voice as I explained to him the itinerary for golf the following week with Barry. He knew I had some reservations about my golf swing as I had not been playing my best at the time. Tony shared with me one last thought before ending our conversation. "KO, glorify God with every shot! Good, bad, or indifferent, glorify God with every shot!" We must do that in all things! In our relationships, our marriage, our parenting, our jobs, our conversations, and in all activities, we indulge in. Do our best, follow through, and glorify God while doing it.

Follow-through is one of the most powerful actions in any field, industry, or sport. We thank God that His Son followed through with the ultimate sacrifice, enabling us to have everlasting life in Heaven with Him, as well as with those who have gone before us. In golf, the ascent or follow-through in a golf shot marks the completion of the swing and emphasizes a point of accuracy. It reinforces the direction and trajectory of the flight of a golf ball. It validates your commitment to your swing and every swing phase before it. Finish the swing!

Can you imagine, on so many levels and so many ideas, the benefits we enjoy as humans if the creators of inventions had not followed through on any of the tasks required to complete their respective ideas, thoughts, and ultimately their projects for their creations?

Whether it was the light bulb by Thomas Edison, the airplane by the Wright Brothers, or more recent inventions like Facebook, Instagram, or electric vehicles, life would be profoundly different for all of us.

How does "follow through" resonate with you in terms of your identity and your current profession? How has it impacted you in both a positive or negative way, influencing your self-worth and how others perceive you?

What about when a person doesn't follow through on their commitment to you, whether it's a personal or professional commitment that holds significant importance? It's a challenge for me, and probably for most people, to overlook someone who fails to fulfill a commitment they made to us. Depending on the importance of that commitment, it can strain a relationship and potentially have consequences in other areas as well. Follow through is one of the most critical aspects of life across various walks and industries. Follow through means to persist with an action or task until it reaches its conclusion. In sports, such as golf, it entails continuing one's movement after the ball has been struck.

What does it mean to follow through in our faith? Perhaps Hebrews 10:36 explains it best: *"You need to persevere so that when you have done the will of God, you will receive what he has promised."* When we follow through and don't quit, He promises to honor our efforts. The key to success is often hidden from the world, but obvious to us. Deep in my heart, I attribute my success in all areas of life to God's blessings on me and my family through His grace and mercy, despite my sins and shortcomings. Philippians 4:19 says, *"And my God will supply every need of yours according to his riches in glory in Christ Jesus."* I can assure you, at the ripe age of fifty, He has provided all of my needs one hundred percent. It would require another book to walk you through all what He has provided for me and my family. It's one of many promises God has provided and it gives me rest.

We've all depended on mantras in the most intense life experiences. Through words of encouragement from a friend, or perhaps someone you don't know:

"Push through it."

"Finish strong."

"Run through the finish line!"

These mantras may have even resonated within your mind and heart as a soft voice from God's Holy Spirit. It is your spirit being fed and inspired by the eternal encouragement from God in moments of vulnerability and weakness. I wonder if these mantras stem from Philippians 3:14, where Paul says, *"I press on to reach the end of the race and receive the heavenly prize for which God, through Christ Jesus, is calling us?"* In all cases, God will provide you the resources and strength to do it. I love how Paul articulates it in 2 Corinthians 12:9-11: *"But he said to me, 'My grace is sufficient for you, for my power*

is made perfect in weakness.' Therefore, I will boast all the more
gladly about my weaknesses, so that Christ's power may rest on me.
That's why, for Christ's sake, I delight in weaknesses, in insults,
in hardships, in persecutions, in difficulties. For when I am weak,
then I am strong."* If I had the opportunity to rewrite this
scripture, I would place exclamation marks on every sentence.
It is the story of Paul's life, my life, and maybe even your life.

Not only will we finish our golf swing with strength in
the follow-through, but let's also strive to follow through on
our dreams, finding joy while learning from our weaknesses
and failures. Let's persevere through insults, hardships, and
criticism, knowing that God protects us and guides us through
those tough moments. As it's written in 2 Timothy 4:7, *"I
have fought the good fight, I have finished the race, I have kept
the faith."* I admire how one of my mentors shared this with
me, and I wholeheartedly embrace this perspective: "When
it's all said and done, and I have followed through, and when
the dust settles, you will find me on my knees with my hands
up, looking up to God, giving Him all the glory!"

What accomplishments have you completed this past year?

_____

_____

_____

_____

What goals do you have that are still underway? _____

_____

_____

_____

_____

What projects have you not completed and why not? List those reasons below along with lessons learned from those experiences. _____

_____

_____

_____

_____

MEET ME BACK INSIDE THE CLUBHOUSE

Validate Your Scorecard

*"That the generation to come might know, even the
children yet to be born, That they may arise and tell
them to their children."*
—Psalm 78:6

"What did you shoot?" If you're a golfer, you've been
asked this question hundreds of times. People in
the clubhouse want to know. I recall in 2016, a late, dear
friend of mine, Jeff Lawson, invited me to an exclusive club,
Madison Golf Club in LaQuinta, California. The course was
a championship course—immaculate, well-groomed, and
simply pristine. Several PGA Tour players were members,
such as Phil Mickelson and Freddie Couples. Phil held the

record from the #2 tee box, while another PGA player, Ben Crane, held the record from the #1 tees, which played over 7,400 yards in length and was a par 72.

My twin brother, Kevin, and I met our friend, a member of The Madison Club, and his friend, Paul Imondi, for a foursome. At the time, Paul was a PGA professional, touring on the Korn Ferry tour and had quite a talent. In other words, he was a great golfer. We teed off just like any other day on a normal round of golf, playing from the #1 tees. It was an amazing experience, complete with a caddie to guide us through the round, informing us where to hit and where not to.

As we continued playing, Kevin and I learned on the 10th hole that our new friend, Paul, was 5 under par on the front nine. Our eyes widened, and our mouths fell open. "Wow!" That was all we could say. We watched Paul more closely, marveling at his ball striking. The course record at that time was 64, or 8 under par, set by Ben. Paul proceeded to birdie holes 10 through 13 and was 9 under par. He was now on pace to beat the record by one stroke. Madison staff members started coming out on the course to watch him play. The word was out—he was going for the record. It was the craziest thing ever. The music that had been playing loudly throughout the entire round was now reduced to silence.

Out of the blue, Paul lit up a cigarette, even though he had quit smoking five years earlier. It was intense for him, and for all of us watching, taking it all in.

Paul parred the 14th through the 16th hole, and now he was on the 17th hole, a par 3, 235 yards. He struck a 2-iron nicely to hit the green 65 feet from the flagstick but three-putted to bogey the hole. He was now at 8 under par, still on pace to tie the record.

As Paul stood on the 18th tee box, par 5, he only needed a birdie to break the record, worst case a par to tie. He hit the fairway off the tee and found the fairway with his second shot. His solid iron shot hit the green in regulation. He grabbed his putter and struck the ball for his fourth shot, leaving himself a two-footer for par.

Without hesitation, Paul walked up to the ball and tapped it in, only to have it horseshoe back to him, resulting in a miss and a bogey. His caddie looked at him with folded arms and said out loud, "That's a bogey!" He missed the record by one stroke. It was epic, but also a bit sad.

As we made our way back to the clubhouse, the question arose, as it usually does, "What did you shoot?"

It's standard procedure after every PGA tournament for the paired groups to exchange their respective scorecards with one another to validate the scores. Each individual acts as a witness and must sign the other's scorecard, confirming that their opponent indeed scored what they reported. I had the honor of witnessing an amazing round by a new friend, who remains a friend to this day. I would have signed that scorecard without hesitation. But I didn't just witness Paul's golfing skills; I also saw who he was as a person.

Paul is soft-spoken, polite, kind, and respectful, just to briefly describe him. What's even more attractive about Paul, and why our friendship endures, is that he is a man of God with Christ-like characteristics. His faith was apparent on the course that day.

In over four hours spent on a golf course, whether with strangers, new friends, or old, what legacy will you leave with those individuals? Throughout this book, we've explored who I am, what I strive to encourage and inspire in others when I engage with them, and how I can be of assistance to anyone seeking a purposeful and joyful life. How would you like to be remembered? Who will validate the scorecard of your life? What is being said about you today, and what will be said after you're gone?

They call me KO. I'm a man of God who loves his family, loves people, and loves the game of golf. If you know me, you should have no trouble affirming that these characteristics accurately reflect my life. At least that is my hope and what I strive to do. I pray we all are doing our best to use God's gift He's given us in our perspective capacities, and witness to and serve others.

As we reconvene in the clubhouse and reflect on our time together during our metaphorical 18 holes of applying golf principles and swing mechanics to life, let's continue to fight the good fight, finish the race, and keep the faith. Just as Paul encourages us in Galatians 6:9: *"Let us not get tired of doing good, for at just the right time we will reap a harvest of blessing if we do not give up."*

Take life one day at a time, spend time with God, and surround yourself with a trustworthy group of family and friends with whom you can share your vision. God will sustain you. I hope the insights shared through these 18 metaphoric holes of golf and reflections on faith, along with the outlined principles, prove valuable in guiding you towards becoming the person you aspire to be and achieving your life goals. Share your dreams with God, and watch Him work through you. I'm certain that people are watching! God bless you and Godspeed!

GLOSSARY

Golf Clubhouse—A facility located on a golf course that serves as a central gathering place for players and visitors. It typically provides amenities such as locker rooms, dining areas, a pro shop, and sometimes even event or meeting spaces. Golfers often use the clubhouse to check in before a round, socialize, relax, and enjoy refreshments after their game.

Golf Range—Also known as a driving range, it is a practice facility for golfers to work on their swings and shots. It usually includes a teeing area with multiple hitting stations, along with targets at various distances to help golfers practice their accuracy and distance control. Golfers hit golf balls at the range to refine their skills and improve their game.

Golf Club Driver—A type of golf club designed for hitting long-distance shots off the tee. Golfers use the driver to achieve the longest possible tee shot, aiming to cover significant distances while setting up favorable positions for subsequent shots on the golf course.

Golf Club Irons—A type of golf club designed for shots that require accuracy and control, typically from shorter distances than those covered by drivers. They have a flat clubface with grooves that help impart spin on the ball for better control. Irons are numbered from 1 to 9, with lower numbers having lower lofts and longer shafts for long shots, while higher numbers have higher lofts and shorter shafts suitable for shorter approach shots. There are also pitching wedges and sand wedges, which are considered irons and are used for shots near the green and out of bunkers, respectively.

Fade Golf Shot—A type of ball flight that curves gently from left to right (for a right-handed golfer) or right to left (for a left-handed golfer). This shot is intentionally executed by manipulating the clubface and swing path to create a controlled slice or cut spin on the ball. A fade is often used to navigate around obstacles, stay in play, or position the ball favorably on the fairway. It is distinct from a draw shot, which curves in the opposite direction.

Fairway—The closely-mowed and well-maintained area of grass between the tee box and the putting green. It provides a clear and even surface for golfers to play their shots after the tee shot and before reaching the green. Fairways are typically wider than the rough (the longer grass that borders the fairway) and offer a more predictable surface for golfers to hit their approach shots, aiming for better accuracy and distance control.

Rough—Areas of longer, thicker grass that are adjacent to the fairways and greens. It is intentionally left to grow higher and is less manicured than the fairway. Golfers who hit their shots off-target might find themselves in the rough, making their next shots more challenging due to the difficulty of controlling the ball from the thicker grass. The rough adds an element of difficulty to the game and requires players to adjust their approach based on the lie and conditions of the ball in that area.

Green—highly manicured, smooth, and precisely maintained areas where the hole is located for putting. Golfers complete a hole by attempting to sink the ball into the hole on the green with as few strokes as possible. The texture and speed of the green can vary, influencing the pace and accuracy required for successful putting. Greens are typically the most carefully managed areas of a golf course, as their condition significantly affects the overall playability and enjoyment of the game.

Sand Bunkers—Also known as sand traps, these are hazards strategically placed around the course. They are filled with sand and designed to challenge golfers by adding difficulty to shots. Golfers need to use specific techniques to get the ball out of the bunker and onto the green or fairway. Bunkers come in various shapes and sizes, and their placement often requires golfers to plan their shots carefully to avoid these hazards and optimize their performance.

Penalty—A punishment imposed on a player for violating the rules of the game. Penalties are designed to maintain fairness, integrity, and consistency in the sport. Common rule infractions that result in penalties include hitting the ball out of bounds, taking an improper drop, moving the ball improperly, and not following procedures related to hazards and bunkers. Penalties can vary in severity, with strokes being added to a player's score or requiring the player to replay a shot. The goal of penalties is to ensure that all players adhere to the rules and compete on a level playing field.

Mulligan—A do-over or a second chance that a golfer takes on a shot without incurring any penalty. It's an informal term and not officially recognized in the official rules of golf. Mulligans are typically used when a player hits a poor shot, and they want to replay it without counting the stroke. Mulligans are a way to make the game more relaxed and enjoyable.

Par—A par score in golf refers to the number of strokes an expert golfer is expected to take to complete a hole or a round.

It represents the standard performance level for each hole, and players aim to complete the hole in the same number of strokes as the par score.

Birdie—A birdie score in golf occurs when a player completes a hole in one stroke less than the designated par score for that hole. For instance, if a hole has a par score of 4 and a player takes only 3 strokes to complete it, they have scored a birdie on that hole.

Eagle—An eagle score in golf happens when a player completes a hole in two strokes less than the designated par score for that hole. For example, if a hole has a par score of 5 and a player takes only three strokes to complete it, they have scored an eagle on that hole.

Bogey—A bogey score in golf occurs when a player completes a hole in one stroke over the par score designated for that hole. For instance, if a hole has a par score of 4 and a player takes five strokes to complete it, they have scored a bogey on that hole.

Double Bogey—A double bogey score in golf happens when a player completes a hole in two strokes over the designated par score for that hole. For example, if a hole has a par score of 3 and a player takes five strokes to finish it, they have scored a double bogey on that hole.

Triple Bogey – Occurs when a player takes three strokes more than the listed par for a particu-lar hole. For example, if a hole is a par 4, and a player takes seven strokes to complete it, they have scored a triple bogey.

About the Author

Kerwin Owens, a true child of God, stands as a devoted husband to his beloved Demetris for over two decades and a loving father to three wonderful children: Devin, Demi, and Kennedy. His journey has been marked by extraordinary accomplishments, holding a Bachelor of Science degree in Electrical Engineering from Prairie View A&M University. Notably, he was named Most Valuable Player in his junior year of college football, attracting the attention of multiple professional NFL and CFL teams.

Yet, Kerwin's story is more than a tale of academic and athletic success. His remarkable tenacity to make a lasting impact, his unwavering love for people, and his inherent leadership qualities have led him to hold significant leadership positions for over twenty years in prestigious Fortune 500 companies, both in the automotive and aerospace and defense sectors. He's been a globe-trotter, guiding numerous organizations towards improvement through his expertise in Quality Engineering.

Parallel to his corporate journey, Kerwin has been a beacon of guidance and support for individuals across various industries. He has served as a personal and professional coach, helping people harness their God-given gifts, talents, and passions to live out their purposes. Whether you're a corporate executive or an integral part of your family, Kerwin can lead you through self-discovery, identification, and growth in four key dimensions of life: Emotional, Relational, Physical, and Spiritual.

What truly sets Kerwin apart is his profound impact on diverse backgrounds and professions, including law, finance, medical, professional sports, and family dynamics. Through warm, safe, non-judgmental, and non-critical conversations, he has encouraged and inspired countless individuals. His wisdom has made him a sought-after speaker at non-profit organizations, educational institutions, and events worldwide, motivating and inspiring both individuals and teams on a range of topics.

Additionally, upon request, Kerwin offers his wisdom to officiate weddings and counsel couples preparing for marriage or seeking to enhance their relationships. His dedication extends beyond his professional life, as he finds joy in spending time with God, his cherished family, and building enduring relationships.

In the spirit of Matthew 25:40, Kerwin embodies the principle that every act of kindness to our fellow human beings is a reflection of our love and service to a higher purpose.

And it states: "*And the King will say, 'For sure, I tell you, because you did it to one of the least of these My brothers, you have done it to Me.'*"

Acknowledgments

Writing this book has been one of the most amazing journeys and accomplishments in my life. As I reflect on my journey since childhood, my story began while sitting in church listening to my grandfather, Rufus Guillory, preach, teach, and describe God and His son, Jesus, every Sunday over the span of my childhood and further into my young adult life. What he taught me, along with my parents, shows up in the writing of "Follow Through." My grandfather, my dad, along with many of my loved ones and extended family and friends, have completed their follow-through. They've finished their assignments. The experiences and learnings from watching them over the years inspired me to write what I believe are the most important key aspects of follow-through, hoping to inspire and encourage many others.

I'd like to give a big thank you to my dad and mom, Mr. and Mrs. Winfred and Jeroldine Owens, for instilling in me the understanding that I can achieve all my desires with God's blessing and His hands in it.

I gratefully acknowledge the unwavering support of my wife, Demetris, who consistently inspires me to be all that I can be through her motivation and encouragement in the most uniquely impactful ways that I will never forget. My three children, Devin, Demi, and Kennedy, have been remarkably supportive and patient, listening to me talk, helping me write, and providing valuable insights, some of which I share in this book. It has been simply amazing, and I will forever be grateful for who you are. It is one of the many significant reasons I wake up every day to watch you grow and make indelible marks on this earth wherever you are in your lives. Demetris, Devin, Demi, and Kennedy, you are my greatest blessing!

I dedicate this work to the pursuit of excellence, drawing inspiration from some of the members of my own personal board of directors who have advised me in the writing of this book: Don Johnson, Mickey Washington, Philip June, and Shelby Miller. To the countless Bible studies over the span of eleven years, I appreciate the fellowship of Winfred Owens, Kevin Owens, Byron Gallien, Kyu Ho, Morgan Trent, and others. Those engagements and studying God's Word have made a significant difference in my life. Thank you very much, Tony Jonas, Lynn Stone, and Jeff Shetler, for many nights delving into the Bible and dissecting golf for many years, where I have strengthened both my faith and my golf game. There are many other friends and family members unnamed who have created experiences and memories for a lifetime whom I'll never forget. Thank you! Let's continue to create! You know who you are.

A special thanks to Liz Gilder, Tiara Nacole, Marcela Foreman, and Spencer Foreman. Thank you, Anna Baldwin. It was your listening to one of my chapters and encouraging

www.ingramcontent.com/pod-product-compliance
Lightning Source LLC
Chambersburg PA
CBHW020449130626
46549CB00001B/351

words afterwards that moved me to think about those who are lost. I dedicate the "Mulligan" hole to you. A ton of gratitude and appreciation for Mr. and Mrs. Richard and Deryl Holden for the prayers and support in countless ways. Thank you to Mr. and Mrs. Julian and Jocelyn Hobdy for their spiritual support.

As well as my brother-in-law Robert and Stacey Holden for hosting my family and me in their home during such a memorable hot summer in Texas for a couple of months down the stretch as I finished this book. Their warm hospitality through food and comfort was unmatched!

A very special thanks to my editor, Jessica Tilles, for her patience and understanding during this journey of writing.

And God, I truly appreciate your partnership and inspiration through your Word and Holy Spirit, and our amazing time together writing this book. I give you all the glory and honor for the thoughts, the scriptures you provided, and undoubtedly 100% of the ability to follow through on this assignment. Without you, it is impossible to have written in this way. You are and will forever be my God!